Value

Value

Frederick Harry Pitts

polity

First published in 2021 by Polity Press

Polity Press
65 Bridge Street
Cambridge CB2 1UR, UK

Polity Press
101 Station Landing
Suite 300
Medford, MA 02155, USA

ISBN-13: 978-1-5095-3565-1
ISBN-13: 978-1-5095-3566-8 (pb)

A catalogue record for this book is available from the British Library.

Library of Congress Cataloging-in-Publication Data

Names: Pitts, Frederick Harry, author.
Title: Value / Frederick Harry Pitts.
Description: Cambridge, UK ; Medford, MA : Polity Press, 2021. | Series: What is political economy? | Includes bibliographical references and index. | Summary: "Why are some things worth more than others? A leading expert investigates"-- Provided by publisher.
Identifiers: LCCN 2020024385 (print) | LCCN 2020024386 (ebook) | ISBN 9781509535651 (hardback) | ISBN 9781509535668 (paperback) | ISBN 9781509535675 (epub)
Subjects: LCSH: Value. | Economics.
Classification: LCC HB201 .P55 2021 (print) | LCC HB201 (ebook) | DDC 338.5/21--dc23
LC record available at https://lccn.loc.gov/2020024385
LC ebook record available at https://lccn.loc.gov/2020024386

Typeset in 10.5 on 12pt Sabon
by Fakenham Prepress Solutions, Fakenham, Norfolk NR21 8NL
Printed and bound in Great Britain by CPI Group (UK) Ltd, Croydon

For further information on Polity, visit our website:
politybooks.com

To Nico

Contents

Introduction

This book introduces how the idea of value has been understood within political economy, and the social and political implications of its different interpretations. The book traverses Aristotle, mercantilism, the classical political economy of Smith and Ricardo, Marxism, marginal utility theory and its neoclassical descendants, institutionalist economics and the sociology of valuation. Surveying the most important conceptualizations of value, the book considers issues such as what makes one thing exchangeable with another, the relationship between value and price, and the ascription of value creation to some activities over others. The book transcends economic explanations alone, exploring the social and political significance of decisions made about what things are worth, and the people and processes involved in their creation.

A closed case for much of mainstream economic thinking, the issue of value is a pressing one because it exposes the tension at the heart of the social and political processes that render all things equivalent and comparable under the single measure of price. These processes are increasingly at stake politically. National populists content to sacrifice economic rationality for an emotional politics of belonging; anti-'globalist' protectionisms fencing value back within borders; anti-austerity social movements protesting the hunger for gold of high finance; the establishment of so-called 'real' economies centred on alternative currencies and business models that purport to keep wealth within localities – all lay claim to a critique of the social and political processes through which capital, states and other actors value and price the world around us. But only further populist discontent and frustration will follow the failure of this constellation of political tendencies to grasp what really underpins a society that knows the price of everything and the value of nothing.

Value theory, the book shows, provides a better footing to grasp the social forms and relations with which the present political moment fumbles. In navigating value, the book is indebted to Marx's critique of political economy, which, rather than as an alternative economics or political economy, is treated here as a critical theory of society itself.[1] As opposed to *critical* theory, traditional or mainstream theory does not go beyond the way things appear – the forms in which human social relations are mediated, such as labour, capital, money and the state.[2] It takes these things for granted, and presents them as natural or static. In some cases, it purports to solve practical problems pertaining to them; in others, it makes moral arguments about the justice or ethics of a given social formation. Archetypal of this tradition is the classical political economy of Adam Smith and David Ricardo – which broke new ground by understanding labour, capital, value and the relationship between them. Well before the rise of pure economics, classical political economy highlighted the idiosyncrasies of a system where a surplus accrues from the transaction of apparently equivalent commodities. Tracing this surplus back to the labour process, political economy embedded economic phenomena within social relations of power and domination. But it did not adequately enquire as to the conditions of possibility and reproduction of historically peculiar products of human practice such as commodities and money.

It was left to Marx, with his critique of political economy, to explore how the forms of economic objectivity assumed by classical political economy were grounded in a set of antagonistic social relations and systemic structures that compel individuals to act in certain ways. Critical theory, unlike traditional theory, recognizes and relativizes its own theoretical claims and those of others as a part of the social world they theorize. Marx's immanent critique confronted classical political economy on this basis, as a part of the society it studied, proceeding through the tales that capitalism told about itself in its works of theory to the underlying social constitution they expressed.

The rebranding of economics as a science introduced a separation between politics and economy unthinkable to the political economy that preceded it, and this has coloured the reception of value theory since. The intellectual historian Philip Mirowski, whose work we return to throughout this book, acerbically observes that economists presume an impossible ability to model the reality of economic life from a safe scientific distance, but are themselves implicated in the 'cultural movements of their time or the metaphors used to rationalize the physical and social worlds'.[3] As Marx captured, even the most seemingly objective ideas about society are themselves part and parcel of that society and its reproduction.

In this sense, value theory is no mere academic exercise. The 'objective' theories of value that reigned supreme until the late nineteenth century stressed labour's role in production, and policed a boundary between productive and unproductive sectors of the economy that had real impact on decisions made about investment, policy and income distribution, as well as the politics of social division in ascendant capitalist societies.[4] Later, 'subjective' theories of value in neoclassical economics centred on preferences, including those of workers in choosing labour over leisure depending on the right incentives. Whilst freeing value theory from 'productivist' principles centring solely on the sphere of production to capture better the relational character of value in the sphere of consumption, valid substantialist insights, which highlight the role of the employment relationship in the constitution of value, were cast aside. The persuasiveness of subjective theories of value was aided by the claims to scientific status inherent in neoclassical economics. One of the great misfortunes of subjective theories of value, Mariana Mazzucato notes, is how:

In the intellectual world, economists wanted to make their discipline seem 'scientific' – more like physics and less like sociology – with the result that they dispensed with its earlier political and social connotations ... while economics students used to get a rich and varied education in the idea of value, learning what different schools of economic thought had to say about it, today they are taught only that value is determined by the dynamics of price, due to scarcity and preferences.[5]

There is, of course, some sense in this schooling, insofar as these ideas, true or not, really do structure the way things are valued – or at least how value is calculated – in capitalist society. Marginalist utility theory still structures how governments govern, investors invest and businesses do business.[6] In this way, theories of value have a performative effect and one might just as well learn to use the master's tools as any others. Nonetheless, the essence of a critical method is to think through and against the grain of the way things are to create the potential of an alternative. However much neoclassical economics captures or sculpts the reality of economic life in contemporary capitalism, it is insufficient to simply stop there. It is the contention of this book that, in order to do this, a leap must be made from economic to social theories of value.

* * * *

The problem of value, as Robert Heilbroner puts it, represents 'the effort to tie the surface phenomena of economic life to some inner structure or order'.[7] Aristotle inaugurated the study of this problematic, inquiring after how the 'equalization of unlike objects as commodities ... requires an arbitrary and conventional means of equalization: in other words, a notion of value'.[8] In the modern age, meanwhile, political economy confronted the problem of value by seeking 'the basis of just price in a non-absolute world', rapidly freeing itself from royal or divine determination.[9] We can follow Heilbroner in broadly identifying 'five distinct attempts to unravel the value problematic': substantialism, the cost-of-production approach, Marx's theory of value, utility theory and the normative theory of value. These map roughly onto Mirowski's demarcation between conservation or *substance* theories of value, comprising substantialism and cost of production; *field* theories of value, which span Marx and utility theory; and the *social* theory of value, of which Heilbroner seems to be speaking too in his delineation of the 'normative' institutionalist approach to value.[10] This book broadly tracks this typology, covering each of these strands in turn, as well as some others along the way.

Chapter 1, 'Value as Substance', considers theories of value that posit a conserved substance in the commodity itself, typically put there by labour. This idea develops through so-called 'balance of trade' mercantilism based on trade and competition between nations, which vied with physiocratic accounts of the productive centrality of agriculture to nascent capitalist economies. It blossoms in classical political economy and its focus on the surplus, before reaching its climax in the critique of political economy by Marx, who moved beyond market exchange to confront the classed dynamics of the workplace in determining the production and distribution of value.

Chapter 2, 'Value as Relation', considers the development of so-called 'field' theories of value that situate value not in any thing or activity but rather in the money-mediated relationship between them. First, we survey the contribution of 'free trade' mercantilists and the work of Samuel Bailey, before using the so-called 'new reading' of Marx to demonstrate how the full development of the latter's value theory breaks with substantialist accounts of the production of value, stressing instead the sphere of circulation and the moment of monetary exchange in ascribing value to products of labour. This places Marx on the path to a proto-marginalist 'subjective' theory of value – a historically decisive break with the 'objective' theories of value associated with prior political economy.

Chapter 3, 'Value as Utility', examines the development of the relational 'field' theory of value marginalist utility theory. We first explore its foundations and political imperatives through the work of Bernoulli and Bentham, before a discussion of its central unit of analysis, the 'util'. Drawing on critical reconstructions in the work of institutionalists such as Mirowski, we identify utility theory's incomplete break with a concept of substance. Finally, we explore, through a consideration of the so-called 'Weber–Fechner' debate, issues in the marginalist tradition around the measurability of marginal utility. Whilst utility theory has some advantages, moving from a production-based standpoint to include other moments of consumption and exchange within the determination of value, its individualized and asocial view of capitalist society leaves significant conceptual gaps with problematic real-life consequences.

Chapter 4, 'Value and Institutions', surveys how 'social' and 'normative' theories of value plug gaps inherent in other approaches to value. We first explore the 'normative' theory of value inaugurated with Aristotle, before charting the development of the 'social' theory associated with institutionalists like Thorstein Veblen and John Commons, before moving on to the more recent 'power' theory of value promoted in the work of Jonathan Nitzan and Shimshon Bichler. We then discuss the increasingly significant 'Sociology of Valuation and Evaluation' – specifically, how social and political processes of valuation are theorized in the work of Arjun Appadurai, and the 'valuation studies' that develop from his work an analysis of the 'regimes of value' enacted in so-called 'market devices', as well as the 'cultural economy' approach influenced by Michel Callon and Pierre Bourdieu. Continuing a focus on the 'performativity' of both value and theories of it, we use the work of Mazzucato to explore the past and present politics of productiveness and unproductiveness that both influence the development of different theories of value and represent their real-world outcome.

Chapter 5, 'Value as Struggle', revisits aspects of both the 'substantialist' and the 'relational' Marx introduced in the first and second chapters, using open Marxism and autonomist Marxism to delve deeper to unfold the historical constitution of value in a set of classed, gendered and racialized social relations based on the separation of individuals from the independent means to reproduce the conditions of living, and how the dual character of labour as concrete and abstract within the production process itself represents the terrain for class struggle over the form and content of work and value in capitalist society.

Chapter 6, 'Value in Crisis', closes the book by considering the possible futures of value in a financialized economy based on modes of 'immaterial' production. The 'postoperaist' school of Italian post-Marxism proposes a crisis in the law of value, wherein the value produced by contemporary digital labour exceeds the capacity of capital to capture it through means such as financialization. We conclude by insisting on the persistence of value in spite of its purported 'crisis' – if not as an economic category, then as a subject of social and political struggle that will rage into a new decade of populism, technological change and, now, at the time of writing this introduction, pandemic.

* * * *

Finally, some acknowledgements. This book brings together threads from a decade-long empirical and theoretical interest in value, but the initial spark for much of the work represented here was a project led by Lee Marshall of the University of Bristol on 'The Value of Music in the Digital Age', funded by the Faculty of Social Sciences and Law. My thanks go to Lee for his input and support with the original mapping of, and early work on, the book that followed. I have also learnt a great deal from conversation and collaboration on the topic of value with other colleagues and friends over the past years – in particular, Matt Bolton, Jon Cruddas, Ana Dinerstein and Patrizia Zanoni. Sincere thanks are also due to George Owers at Polity for suggesting that I write the book in the first place, and the excellent editorial support received thereafter from him and his team. In particular, I would like to thank two anonymous reviewers for their incredibly generous and helpful comments on the manuscript at an earlier stage. All the usual disclaimers apply, especially seeing as I did not have the space to respond to their recommendations in full. The book is dedicated to my youngest daughter Nico – funnily enough, not the first baby in recent family history to be born in the breathing space between submission and revision of a book I was writing. With that in mind, I would like to thank my partner and children for bearing with me in the final throes of writing and revising the book amidst the strange and slightly crazed lockdown days of the first half of 2020. The book was written before the pandemic hit, but the debates raging in its wake – about the value of previously undervalued forms of work, or the value of human life and health versus the value of continuing economic activity – will only intensify in the inevitable crisis to come, sharpening the political and material significance of the issues discussed in the pages that follow.

1
Value as Substance

Substantialist approaches to value posit the labour content of a good or service as 'an order-bestowing force', as opposed to anything external to it.[1] Substantialist theories of value see value as carried and conserved within things, either inhering within the things themselves or inserted there by the labour that created them. They rest on a series of defining positions: the ascription of a natural basis to economic value; the suggestion that value is conserved from the production through to the exchange of products; the 'reification' of the economy as an orderly 'law-governed structure' akin to nature; the proposal of an 'invariant standard' of value; the policing of a boundary between activities productive and unproductive of value; the conviction that the sphere of production is where value is determined; and the resulting 'relegation' of money to a purely 'epiphenomenal status' expressive of embodied labour.[2] As with so much else in value theory, we can trace this line of interpretation to Aristotle, who located in labour a common element underlying the mystery of the equivalent exchange of diverse goods.[3]

In the modern age, theories of value mimicked the development of Western physics.[4] When the physics of energy conservation was the only science available, the first stirrings of substantialism in 'balance of trade' mercantilism took on the Cartesian insight that motion is an 'embodied substance ... passed about from body to body by means of collision', reifying value as a substance 'conserved in the activity of trade to provide structural stability to prices and differentially specified in the process of production'.[5] Taking this analogy forwards, where the substantialist approach really comes alive is in the work of the physiocrats and, later, the classical political economists. In the *Wealth of Nations*, Adam Smith suggests that 'It is natural that what is usually the produce of two days' or two hours' labour, should be worth double of what is usually the produce of one day's or one hour's labour', a position later taken up by David Ricardo and, to some extent, Karl Marx.[6]

From mercantilism onwards, the trajectory of substantialism and associated 'objective' theories of value from the seventeenth century was also deeply imbricated in social and political shifts, and served the purposes of different actors at different times in different places, with consequences by turns reformist, reactionary and revolutionary. Mercantilism buttressed the social power of the rising merchant class with a zero-sum understanding of value as bound within national borders in the face of expanding international trade; physiocracy buttressed the power of agriculturalists against mercantile interests; classical political economy, the power of industrialists against feudal remnants; and Marx's version of the labour theory of value, the power of the increasingly assertive proletariat against the industrialists. Today, the national populist tenor of the times grants conservationist appreciations of value as a zero-sum game or substance in time and space fresh political potency, rendering the study of substance theories of value newly relevant. The present-day salience of such thinking shows that the problem of value is by no means a drily academic topic, but one that touches everyday life and current affairs.

Mercantilism and Physiocracy

Substantialist theories of value first had real-world economic and political impact through so-called 'balance of trade' mercantilism, the 'first appearance of a conservation principle in Western economic thought'.[7] Mercantilism reacted to the shifting political economy of sixteenth- and seventeenth-century colonialism, wherein trade expanded and vast amounts of precious metals were extracted from colonies and transformed into currency. The latter came to convey wealth and prosperity, and the 'production boundary' between productive and unproductive was redrawn around 'whoever bought, owned and controlled' its supply. Where income was greater than expenditure, an enterprise was deemed productive, and those who drew down on this surplus as consumers without producing were deemed unproductive.[8]

The mercantilist understanding of the economy – which reappears today in the return of protectionist nationalisms – suggested that a system of equivalent exchange must always mean, in the words of Francis Bacon, that 'whatever is somewhere gotten is somewhere lost', justifying inter-country rivalry on the basis that 'trade is a zero-sum game'.[9] Value is here taken to be something conserved, and, to the extent that the exchange in which it features is conducted with the national currency, containable within the borders of the state from which it arose. Hence, the positive trade balance – back on the lips of the post-liberal right today – comes to represent the conservation and augmentation of the value substance.

Another element of classical substantialism that crops up in the intellectual imaginary of contemporary populisms of both right and left is the positioning of sections of the economy that are 'productive' of value against those that are 'unproductive' of value. Such a distinction is intrinsic to theories of value that rest on a 'conservation principle'. No substantialism can successfully free itself of the presumption of the unproductiveness of one economic activity or another, because 'the imposition of conservation principles in the context of a substance theory of value essentially dictates the existence of such categories'. The French physiocrats 'were the first to make the postulation of unproductive sectors a hallmark of their analysis', and from this it 'became the hallmark of a substance theory of value'.[10]

The physiocrats were a mid-eighteenth-century school that sprang from the court of Louis XV in France, mainly gathered around the physician and royal advisor François Quesnay. Quesnay's medical practice inspired a 'metabolic' vision of the economy, and specifically the role of agriculture within it. Quesnay was frustrated with the mercantilist policies of the French monarchy, which focused on trade and fundraising for military expenditure, rather than what he saw as the 'productive' agricultural sector.[11] The physiocratic distinction of productive from unproductive had political implications, insofar as the 'almost complete identification of productivity with the agricultural sector had an overriding aim. Their restrictive production boundary gave the landed aristocracy ammunition to use against mercantilism, which favoured the merchant class, and fitted an agricultural society better than an industrial one.'[12] For a physiocrat such as Boisguillebert, the true value of things resided in the amount of labour-time that is expended in the production of the particular commodity, whilst the money that expressed different quantities of value in exchange 'disturbs the natural equilibrium or the harmony of the exchange of commodities'. This is, in part, a result of the historical circumstances in which Boisguillebert operated, whereby the court of Louis XIV was characterized by a 'blindly destructive greed for gold'.[13] In language that invites evident parallels with present populist discourse, Boisguillebert referred to finance as a 'black art', championing a return to the 'real economy' long before it became fashionable to do so – indeed, around the time when such a distinction was still halfway plausible.

Assessing the contributions of Boisguillebert and others, Marx attributes to the physiocrats a laudable desire to investigate surplus value and relate it to labour-time, but without having first given thought to the form of value itself. In this way, the physiocrats were guilty of 'discussing a complex form of the problem without having solved its elementary form'. This led to them 'confusing the labour which is materialised in the exchange-value of commodities and measured in time units with the direct physical activity of individuals'.[14]

Smith and Ricardo

With the rise of classical political economy, Smith and Ricardo critiqued the physiocrats on the basis that burgeoning industry could not be accounted for within a framework that placed all productivity in the hands of agriculture.[15] But this merely replaced the active agent in a similarly productivist appraisal of value. For Smith, value represented the time spent by workers in producing the object in which their labour is realized as productive. For Smith, labour was unproductive only when it did not result in an amount of value proportionate to that required to enable workers to subsist. The necessity of some other quantity through which this subsistence could be secured was what led Smith to conceptualize the role of the surplus in characterizing capitalist production. Workers who drew on the surplus to survive, as well as merchants who merely moved goods rather than created them, fell foul of this divide between the productive and the unproductive.[16] Government, too, fell foul of this ideological distinction, the political consequences of which still cascade through capitalist societies today.

But Smith's innovation was to retain an order-bestowing 'substance' embalmed in the product, associated not with direct labour itself but the *cost* of the inputs that contributed to a given thing's production.[17] Smith, for instance, demarcates unproductive labour that 'consists in services, which perish generally in the instant of their performance' – a live musician, for instance – from that which 'fix[es] and realize[s] itself in [a] vendible commodity which can replace the value of the wages and maintenance' of the labour expended in its production.[18] For Smith, value comprised the so-called 'natural' prices of three elements: labour (wages), land (rent) and capital (profit). This has influenced political and sociological approaches to class which associate different classes with the different forms of capital or wealth they possess, and the relative productiveness and unproductiveness this implies. Smith's approach forces us to question the social and political basis by which different groups benefit from the production of certain goods, undermining the apparent neutrality of economic value and ascriptions of worth. But this line of enquiry cannot overcome the circularity it conceals, almost fatal to its capacity to explain value. Wages, rents and profits are themselves prices expressing a value that must itself be explained, a requirement Smith tries unsuccessfully to absolve himself of with reference to the 'natural' value of labour, land and capital. Smith does not establish the 'value structure' behind the cost of production – the historical determination of the value of labour, land and capital, and the particular form in which this value is expressed in wages, rent and profit.[19] In this way, Smithian approaches, right up to present-day pseudo-critiques of the inequities of class society, focus on the distribution of the different kinds of input and revenue drawn from by different actors and class, precisely without considering what needs to be explained: the underpinning, historically specific, *class* relations mediated in these forms of wealth.[20] Whilst Smith captured the class-oriented character of the constitution of value, the underpinning relations were situated not in any social or historical specificity, but rather in a state of naturalized and ahistorical eternity.[21]

Moreover, whilst acknowledging the stratification of society necessary to the system of commodity production, and recognizing the 'significance of labour' in his theory of production costs, Smith incorporated labour only insofar as it cast producers as simple owners of commodities who enter the marketplace eager to exchange commodified portions of their own embodied, objectified labour with others. This process was not contextualized within capitalist society, but seen as an expression of 'direct barter, the spontaneous form of exchange' intrinsic to the human experience.[22] In this ahistorical and asocial fashion, Smith's analysis centred on the commodity as its key principle, labour's significance relating only to its role in commodity production and exchange. Hence, it is not as simple as saying a labour 'substance' determines value in exchange, but rather there is a two-way process in which the one depends upon the other. This introduces a profound ambivalence in Smith's value theory.[23] The value of a commodity expresses the labour embodied in it, whilst at the same time positing the amount of labour its production commands from the labour marketplace – an apparent exchange of equivalent amounts of objectified labour Smith took at face value. Lacking an effective mechanism for explaining the 'determining social matrix' behind this state of affairs, Smith's approach was 'confused' and 'tautological', and ultimately unsuccessful in its attempt to 'overcome the problematic' of value.[24] It was left to Marx to confront capitalist society as the 'immense collection of commodities' Smith describes, and to uncover the secret of labour power concealed within.[25]

* * * *

Smith's contradictions constituted productive contributions to the emergent field of political economy by spurring others to step in and solve them. The circularity of the cost-of-production approach acted as an effective heuristic for Ricardo, who was more successful than Smith in highlighting the potential political and social factors and consequences behind the appearance of value in price. Just as Smith's value theory was based on an ahistorical natural propensity to truck, barter and exchange on the part of humanity, Ricardo also established a naturalistic basis for his theories in the eternal exchange-value-producing character of labour itself. As Marx writes, 'Ricardo's primitive fishermen and primitive hunter are from the outset owners of commodities who exchange their fish and game in proportion to the labour-time which is materialised in these exchange-values.'[26] But, in viewing industrial capitalism as a qualitative realization of these eternal tendencies, Ricardo at least recognized the historical specificity of how a surplus is produced at the level of the employment relationship. Whilst Ricardo holds to the conceptualization of labour as the source of value, by 'conceding to capital a systematic *influence* on price ... irreducible' to labour, he introduces an antagonistic class basis to the value of the things around us, where Smith had only offered harmony.[27] Later, Marx picked up this thread and ran with it.

What Ricardo highlights is the analytical potential of the cost-of-production approach once its circularity is broken. The cost-of-production approach posits no metaphysical abstract order behind value; its virtue is that it takes at face value the price of inputs and relates them to the value of their output. By leaving open the huge logical blindspot of how the inputs acquire their value to begin with, this perspective leaves the field free for inquiries into the constitution of the value of inputs through historical, social, political and ethical processes and modes of contestation, including hierarchies, tastes, laws and customs. The value of the cost-of-production approach, therefore, lies in its circumvention of abstract inquiry in order to root value in a 'skeptical empiricism that looks no farther than those social relationships of power, morality, and perhaps even reason as the basis on which social continuity is grounded and persists'.[28]

Ricardo, more so than Smith, held to a labour theory of value whereby 'the value of a commodity was strictly proportional to the amount of labour time necessary to produce it'. Around this central position, Ricardo, like Smith, set up a productivist divide between nascent industrial production and apparently anachronistic rent-seeking activities, much along the lines of those today who criticize the purportedly 'false' economy of the finance sector in favour of the so-called 'real' economy represented by industry, or the 'rentiership' of platform firms upon the commonwealth of online sharing and cooperation.[29] For Ricardo, rent-seeking noblemen did not produce or reproduce value but merely acted as an unproductive drain on the surplus, or, at best, where merchants and financiers were concerned, redistributed existing value between themselves.[30] On this point, Ricardo is a good example of where value theory has a real political impact. His critique of 'unproductive' sectors of the economy was influential in the transformation and development of the British state away from aristocratic remnants of the feudal mode of production towards the increased power and dynamism of industrialists.

* * * *

The substantialism of Smith and Ricardo is open to critique on several fronts. Well-worn objections note how the value of 'old furniture' and 'old masters' is entirely independent of labour.[31] Indeed, even freshly manufactured products on the market cannot have their value read-off from the amount of embodied labour-time expended in their production, because otherwise 'the capitalist who employed the most workers and the least machinery would make the most profit'.[32] A similar argument is wagered on the basis of utility theory. If twice as much labour contributes to the killing of a beaver than that of a deer, then the beaver will exchange at twice the price of the deer. But this can only hold in the presence of *'maximizing behaviour'* in the first place, 'whether imposed by scarcity or social conditioning', and the necessities of social reproduction inherent in this behaviour impose certain structures of value regardless of the labour expended in the production of the good at hand. Moreover, for the 'deer–beaver exchange rate' to function at all requires 'a prevailing *disutility of labor*', insofar as labour is experienced not as a 'positive pleasure' but an 'onerous task' that must be rewarded in exchange.[33]

Searching deeper into the foundations of embodied labour theories of value, institutionalist Thorstein Veblen associated the flawed 'conservation principles' that informed substantialism with the role of scientific developments in the intellectual life of contemporary society. Veblen sees substance as akin to a kind of 'economic energy' that underpins the ascription of 'equivalence' and 'equilibrium' to the ratio between the expenditure of force in production and the return achieved in the market. This rests on the inappropriate assumptions that 'the orderliness of natural sequence' bestowed by energy conservation in the natural sciences can be applied seamlessly to the social world, and that the scientific principles in themselves capture the reality of the natural world – when they themselves were in fact surpassed by a relational 'field' understanding of energy.[34]

The flaws of applying conservation principles to the relationship between value and embodied labour as an order bestowing force become clear when one considers the issue of price. For substantialist theories of value, labour acts as a means by which things are moved from the natural sphere of pure use value to the market sphere of exchange. But the price its products attract in the market is the only means by which the purported 'order' that labour grants becomes clear. This price can only become apparent with the buying and selling of the goods labour transforms as commodities. Thus, the basis of value in labour is revealed only through a sequence of circumstances that have little to do with labour itself and everything to do with 'the adventitious circumstances of relative scarcity and utility, in which labour plays no role'.[35] Whilst, according to this reasoning, Ricardo was correct to exclude from his considerations of the labour theory of value scarce, rare and non-reproducible items, the wider substantialist tradition has tended to advocate a metaphysical approach to value as something embalmed in objects, regardless of price.[36] But the notion of labour somehow 'embodied' in an object is itself an abstraction, a 'mental convenience' that renders labour 'homogeneous *when plainly it is not*'. In this way, Ricardianism, in common with all substance theories of value, 'impose[s] upon empirical "facts"' theoretical models that bring order, coherence and plausibility to the immediate appearances of phenomena, rather than engaging in the 'theorization of real-world processes' themselves.[37] In so doing, the surface appearances are taken to represent the entirety of the phenomena itself.

This is not to diminish the considerable impact of substantialist approaches to the labour 'embodied' in commodities. The 'calculation' of exchange ratios and rates of profit using input–output figures owes its conceptual foundations to some notion of a substance of value embodied in things themselves. Such a mathematics of value relies upon the judgement that 'the value of a commodity [is] determined by the physical data relating to methods of production rather than vice versa', focusing on 'the determination *of* value rather than the determination *by* value'. But, ultimately, this fundamentally misinterprets the directionality of the relationship between labour and value, insofar as 'it is only through the exchange of products that individual labours are commensurated' and the labour-times socially necessary for their production established. The substantialist embodied-labour perspective, when channelled through the formulas of input–output, 'understand[s] values as mere derivatives of physical quantities required for production'. However, as we will go on to see, 'the social quantification of production requirements' is in actual fact 'posited in the value abstraction' itself.[38]

Marx

Marx himself is often thought of as advocating precisely such a substantialist or 'embodied' position, in his labour theory of value, as that found in the political economy that preceded him. In this account, a commodity's value always stems from the 'labour time necessary in production', and 'labour performed under the command of capital' likewise always 'produces value, regardless of what later happens to the product', the commodity's value differing from its underpinning value substance only due to the artificial fluctuations of supply and demand.[39] From this perspective, Marx holds to a similar set of 'conservation principles', insofar as labour-time extracted in production reappears in the commodity, where it subsists independent of other activities such as trade and circulation, which can only transfer commodities and their values.[40] The presentation of such a reading of value in Marx's work was partly as a result of political expediencies, sitting within a political and theoretical tradition that has staked its analyses and objectives on the power bestowed upon workers to create the value contained in the world of commodities and lay claim to the wealth produced. Regardless, the substantialist approach to value that we find in Marx represents 'the culmination of the substance-theory tradition' – and, we might add, its most sophisticated and forceful rendition.[41]

In his masterwork, *Capital*, Marx 'start[s] from the simplest form of the product of labour' in the society under study, which is that of capitalism.[42] In capitalist society, this product is the commodity. Whilst some, as we will go on to see, have read this as an indication of the primacy of monetary exchange to Marx's understanding of value, a substantialist reading of Marx's value theory would instead suggest that Marx selects the commodity for the same reason as it was the starting point of Smith's analysis: because it is a product of *labour*, which is the true underpinning principle of value.[43] Marx suggests that the commodity is 'the simplest social form in which the labour product is represented in contemporary society'.[44] The commodity matters because *labour* matters. On this account, instead of looking at prices and seeking an explanation of why they are as they are, the aim for Marx was instead to understand the forms that labour takes and what the consequences of these forms might be.[45] Marx stated the importance of a perspective rooted in labour in his engagement with Smith, suggesting that 'As individuals express their life, so they are. What they are, therefore, coincides with their production, both with *what* they produce and *how* they produce.'[46]

Commodities, for Marx, possess a use value and an exchange value. On the market, commodities are equalized where their exchange values are concerned, and differentiated with regard to their use values. The former is what allows the commodity to be exchanged with others; the latter is what makes the commodity attractive as an object of utility or desire.[47] Commodities must be sufficiently different from one another in order to have specific, particular characteristics that render a good or service a worthwhile purchase amongst all the other similar goods and services for sale on the market. For traditional readings of Marx's value theory, this specificity consists in the ability of the labour engaged in production to offer a particular skill or capacity that endows the product of that labour with an individual use value carrying with it a practical, aesthetic or sensual application that makes the product of labour desirable as a commodity in itself. The commodity's use value – its usefulness to the purchaser – therefore pertains to its endowment with a specific characteristic or feature rendering it superior or unique in some way with reference to other products. Exchange value, meanwhile – its power to command money in the market – is the criterion of the exchangeability of one commodity with one another, and dictates the proportion in which this can be done. In order to be considered exchangeable, two or more commodities must possess some common characteristic which brings them into relation with one another. The most immediate way in which two equivalent commodities might be said to be exchangeable is that they are products of human labour. From this flows the notion, common to the substantialist Marx and classical political economy, that value must have something to do with the labour expended in a product's creation.[48]

Commodities are traded not directly with one another, but by means of money. This is most auspiciously because capitalist societies are not societies of independent commodity producers who take the good or service they produce to market. The capitalist system of organizing economic relations is based upon the separation of workers from the means of production through which they would be able to provide themselves with their own commodities. The ownership of the means of production by a class of capitalists concentrates into the hands of this latter class control over the fruits of the process of production. It is therefore the capitalist who oversees and organizes the aggregate efforts of their workforce, who, structured in accordance with a division of labour, are unable to achieve the production of any good or service individually.

It is partly in explaining how this state of affairs came to be that Marx's developed value theory represents a distinctive step both within and beyond substantialism.[49] Specifically, Marx's theory of labour power follows through on the unfulfilled potential of cost-of-production approaches to value by uncovering the historically determinate character of labour power and its value as a stake in the conflict between workers and capitalists. For Marx, at the inception of value is a prior act of valuation conditioned normatively and politically, even if value thereafter is taken to flow as if by osmosis from its substantial foundation. Certain historical preconditions must be in place to render labour as an act not for itself but for exchange, and these must be institutionally reproduced. It is only by virtue of these conditions being in place that labour can be posited a value to begin with, and, from this, a value notionally posited to that in which labour is embodied thereafter.[50]

In embedding the study of value within an account of its prehistory, Marx's labour theory of value surpassed the naturalization of labour and exchange in the work of Smith and Ricardo. This is not to say that Marx's work was free of transhistorical concepts. Marx saw work – in the sense of the human metabolism with nature through which the world around us is transformed into useful things for us to use, wear, eat and so on – as a necessity specific to humans alone, in that we exist, unlike the animal kingdom, at one remove from nature.[51] Unlike the bee which acts upon nature as a matter of instinct, building its hive, humans conceive of designs upon the world before executing them.[52] Nature does not give over easily to human purposes but – with sometimes disastrous consequences – must be made to bend to our will. This is not a 'natural' state of affairs but expresses the development of humankind as a specific sort of social animal that defines itself through its domination and objectification of nature as a means to establish its own subjective presence in the world.[53] Thus, the need to produce the world around us is a constant part of human life. Humans require means of production – tools, machines – to use to do this, and the application of human effort, in the form of work, to accomplish the transformation of nature.

What differentiated Marx's account of the transhistorical character of the human intercourse with nature from Smith and Ricardo's naturalization of human economic life was its critical confrontation with the contemporary mediation of this essence in the historically specific form of *wage labour*. The selling of one's capacity to labour for a wage, Marx suggested, was the result of a social and political process characterized by violence, struggle and the unintended consequences of movements for reform and liberty. Feudalism – in most cases, the mode of production that preceded capitalism – was characterized by a direct relationship of power and dependence between feudal landlords and their tenant serfs. The serf relied on the landlord for the land that they in turn farmed to subsist, with a payment to the landlord as rent. Whilst their freedom was limited, their subsistence was guaranteed, directly or in collaboration and exchange with others. With the bourgeois revolutions of the seventeenth century in countries like England, France and the Netherlands, these relationships were restructured.[54] From a relationship of mutual interdependence and personalized power with the feudal landlord, tenant serfs were cast free, with nothing to call their own but their capacity to work for pay. Deprived of the independent individual or collective means of producing the things they needed to live directly, the rising proletariat were therefore doubly free: free of feudal domination, and free to dispose of their capacity to labour in the labour market for a wage in order to subsist.[55]

For most, the selling of labour power for a wage became the dominant means of reproducing the conditions of life. In order for them to deploy that capacity to labour, means of production were needed, which a combination of new regimes of property and the rule of law, and brute force and violence, had placed in the hands of a rising merchant and industrial class at precisely the time their technological sophistication was accelerating. The ascendant bourgeoisie was therefore placed in a position to acquire the capacity to labour – the 'labour power' – sold by the new proletariat on the newly created market for labour. The consumption of the commodity labour power enabled the bourgeoisie to reproduce the conditions of their business operations, whose success workers depended on in turn, in order to continue being employed. The things produced were the property of the owners of the means of production. The results of production were sold as commodities on the market by means of money. The producers of these goods – the workers – in turn survived by purchasing their means of living with the wages paid for the disposal of the labour power they sold.

It should be noted here that, whilst these political and economic conditions were central to the rise of capitalism and a society that reproduces itself through the valorization of value, this understanding of the evolution of 'free labour' only gets us part of the way. For Marx, at the same time as 'freeing' labour, capitalism is historically and continuingly constituted in various states of unfree labour, including, notably, slavery.[56] Rather than seeing these as a remnant of pre-capitalist modes of production contravening the intrinsically 'free' character of labour in capitalist society, Marx recognized that the revolution in social relations that paved the path for the rise of capitalism implied the exploitation and appropriation associated with plantation slavery and colonialism.[57] Marx observed that 'without slavery you have no cotton; without cotton you have no modern industry', and that 'the veiled slavery of the wage-earners in Europe needed, for its pedestal, slavery pure and simple in the New World'.[58] Likewise, Marx contended that slavery was itself capitalist insofar as it was driven by the valorization process and the pursuit of profit through productivity gains.[59] Unfortunately, this has not stopped subsequent Marxists neglecting or relegating not only the importance of slavery to the analysis of capitalism, but also the racial domination around which slavery was and is organized.[60] Marx's analysis, then, has also been used to locate – as well as class – racism, and specifically anti-blackness, not as an epiphenomenal consequence or superstructural distortion of capitalist social relations, but as a constitutive factor in its development.[61]

* * * *

In Marx's account of the violence and subjugation at the origin and basis of capitalism, then, the development of labour, exchange and value looks very different than it does in the work of the classical political economists. Marx improved upon prior political economy by explaining how a society in which subsistence is mediated by wage labour came about. As we have seen, he did so through an explanation based outside the workplace itself, taking in broader changes in juridical, political and transactional relationships between class actors in the legal sphere, the market and society at large. But it was insufficient simply to stop there, and, having established this state of affairs in *Capital*, Marx took readers beyond the 'realm of Freedom, Equality, Property and Bentham' into the sphere of production to explore the implications of these changes for how work is performed and experienced, and the hidden mechanics and dynamics of value creation in capitalist society.[62] What Marx called the 'valorization process' – the process by which the value invested in production is expanded in pursuit of profit and the reproduction of the conditions for business to continue – compels the process by which labour is bought, sold and engaged in the 'labour process'.[63] Profit, for Marx, arises where the capitalist is able to receive more from the sale of the good or services they produce than they have expended on its production – in other words, from surplus value. In order to understand how this surplus can be raised from the exchange of equivalents, we pick up where Marx's account of the constitution of wage labour in the proletariat's 'double freedom' left off. The individual's labour power must be sold to a willing buyer in possession of the means of production required to put that labour to good use. This labour power presents at the point of sale a purely potential quantity, for which a wage is agreed in order for the willing buyer – the capitalist – to claim its ownership and thus the ability to turn what is merely a potential into actuality. In selling labour power to the capitalist, the individual thus gives over full and sole discretion as to how, when and for how long the labour power can be employed in its next stage of development – as labour in its concrete, practical existence.[64]

The secret of the surplus at first appears inscrutable because the capitalist purchases the commodity labour power at its value.[65] This value is the 'socially necessary' minimum amount of time that the worker must labour to reproduce her labour power so that she might reappear for work the following morning.[66] Yet for a profit to be turned and the value invested valorized, the monetary worth of what they produce must be greater than the employer has outlaid on wages. How can this be so? Marx contends that the commodity of labour power possesses a unique quality when inserted in the labour process and applied to the means of production: it can create more value than it is worth.[67] For Marx, this cannot be determined in the market alone, but rests on a specific set of antagonistic and highly conflictual relationships situated in the labour process itself. This has to do with the way that the time, effort and productivity of workers is managed through organizational and techno-logical means. The contract of employment having been signed, the employer has the power to wield control over the worker they have recruited, but there is no telling what the effectiveness of the labour capacity they have acquired may be in the production process itself – varying in skill or militancy, for instance. A struggle therefore ensues on the part of the employer to extract from that labour power as much effort and productivity as possible in combination with the means of production they own.[68]

For Marx, the production of commodities is divided up into two parts: necessary labour and surplus labour. Translated into time, the first 'necessary' portion has two determinations: the amount of time taken to produce the commodity demanded for sale by the capitalist, as a measure of general human labour in the abstract; and the amount of time the worker takes to produce the commodity in order to reproduce their labour power with the consumption of equivalent commodities through the provision of a wage. This demonstrates the dual nature of necessary labour-time: necessary for the worker, because of their sustenance, and necessary for the capitalist because 'the continued existence of the worker is the basis of that world'.[69]

Whereas the necessary labour-time is that part of the working day where the labourer works 'for himself', what Marx calls *surplus* labour-time is time spent working for the capitalist. Here, labour power is consumed by the capitalist in order to produce surplus value: that part of the value generated from the labour process left over when the worker's recompense and other associated expenses are taken into account. As such, it is in the capitalist's interests to prolong this part of the working day for as long as possible and minimize the proportion of time spent on the reproduction of the worker. By manipulating the length and composition of the working day, the capitalist can secure a greater amount of value from the commodity of labour power than its value at the point of purchase.

This can be done in two main ways, according to Marx: through raising absolute surplus value or relative surplus value. Both centre on the rate of surplus value, or what Marx also called the rate of exploitation: surplus labour divided by necessary labour.[70] If productivity and intensity are given, the rate of surplus value can only be raised by the prolongation of the working day – absolute surplus value – and if the working day is given, the rate of surplus value can only be increased by a shift in the ratio of necessary to surplus labour, achieved by a change in either productivity or intensity – in other words, relative surplus value.[71]

In raising what Marx calls 'absolute surplus value', employers extend the time workers work above and beyond the bare minimum to earn the wage necessary for the repro-duction of their labour power. The employer pays the same but gets more in return. In this context, 'moments are the elements of profit'. The means of production that lie dormant in workplaces overnight demand this, existing only to 'absorb labour'. Starved of this, plant and equipment do not perform their function, constituting a loss to the capitalist. As such, Marx signifies here that 'to appropriate labour during all the 24 hours of the day is the inherent tendency of capitalist production'.[72] With a watchful eye on the clock, times extra-neous to the labour process are carefully cropped. Workers see infinitesimal, yet ever-increasing, portions of their free time eroded at the beginning and end of the day and at break-times, accumulating over the year into a significant surplus under the command of the employer. Such is the capitalist's 'right' as a buyer: the contract of employment signed, the capitalist possesses full discretion over the way in which the commodity at their disposal is used.[73]

But, likewise, it is the labourer's 'right as a seller' to have a set duration to the working day.[74] Although the working day can vary, certain limits do exist that cannot easily be transgressed by capital: firstly, the physical need for the worker to reproduce himself in order to arrive at the factory gates the next morning; and secondly, the 'moral' aspect related to the social standard of satisfaction, associated with spare time away from work, which varies between individual circumstances and social conditions.[75] Where these limits are in place, raising absolute surplus value becomes more difficult for the capitalist. Other means must be found to increase the ratio of surplus to necessary labour, which do not extend the working day outwardly but restructure it internally. This centres on raising what Marx calls 'relative surplus value'.

The prerogative of relative surplus value pertains to the 'curtailment of the necessary labour time, and [with it] the corresponding alteration in the respective lengths of the two components of the working day'.[76] The necessary labour-time can only be lessened by a fall in the value of the labour power that needs reproducing. This implies that the means of subsistence must be produced over a shorter period, through an increase in productivity.[77] By intensifying work and reducing that portion of the day in which the worker labours for her own reproduction, whether through advances in productivity-raising technologies or management regimes, the capitalist can keep the length of the working day the same whilst increasing the proportion of it given over to the production of surplus value. The immediate aim of capital is, thus, less the contraction in labour-time itself as a narrowing of the time necessary within the day for the worker to reproduce themselves, and thus for a set amount of commodities to be produced.[78] The part of the working day 'socially necessary' to the reproduction of both capital and labour is proportionally shortened, whilst the 'surplus' part of the day that belongs to the capitalist and accrues as surplus value is proportionally lengthened, without infringing limits placed upon the length of the working day as a whole. Whilst the practical consequence of these dynamics might appear to be the theft of workers' time, the capitalist, as the buyer of labour power, is simply exerting their legal right to derive as much use value as they can from the commodity they have purchased.[79] And, in deriving use value from one commodity, they hope to profit from the exchange value in which it results, in the sale of another.

Time, thus, represents the means by which all else is calculated in Marx's substantialist schema, and the basis for the surplus that accrues to the capitalist in the form of value. Commodities, for Marx, are to be understood as 'congealed labour-time', and, where the *substance* of value is human labour, the *measure of its magnitude* is nothing other than labour-time.[80] However, it might be said that, if this state of affairs were really the case and labour-time directly determined value, then work conducted at a relaxed pace would be represented in a greater amount of value than more fastidious and efficient efforts.[81] To clarify, Marx himself forewarns against the substantialist pitfall of regarding labour-time as the measure of commodity value whilst in the same instance 'confusing the labour which is materialised in the exchange value of commodities and measured in time units with the direct physical activity of individuals'.[82] This has implications that, as we will see in subsequent chapters, cannot be neatly contained in a substantialist approach to the value problematic.

* * * *

Scholars like Jean Baudrillard have suggested that Marx's critique, in its continuation of themes from classical political economy, remains too close to its object in assuming the standpoint of one of its conceptual poles, labour.[83] Indeed, partly owing to the political expediencies of the time in which Marx was writing, in places he did endow production and labour with a 'revolutionary title of nobility'. This 'productivism', Baudrillard argues, exhibits a tendency to ascribe to production the status of the 'active moment' in the determination of value, and to other moments, such as consumption, a relative and absolute passivity. This concept-ually subordinates '[s]ocial wealth or language, meaning or value, sign or phantasm' to some kind of 'production' at the hands of one or another type of 'labour'. This productivist logic, Baudrillard suggests, mimics that of capitalist society itself in subordinating everything, 'all human material and every contingency of desire and exchange', to the ends of 'value, finality, and production'.[84] Delving into the realm of production brings us no closer to the truth of the matter, Baudrillard asserts, for, 'instead of the shadows of the market place, we are sent to an equally obscure underside of the system: the place of production'.[85] The latter cannot be understood in isolation from its contradictory unity with the sphere of circulation, just as use value has no existence independent of its contradictory unity with exchange value – the each being the precondition of the other – and concrete labour no existence independent of its contradictory unity with abstract labour.[86] However, Baudrillard argues that this did not stop Marx positivizing the first term of each over the other as the underpinning principle of a wider social transformation, remaining mired in the 'repressed side' of the concepts of classical political economy and the capitalist society it sought to describe.[87]

As such, in basing itself in the perspective of production, a part of Marx's critique was left incomplete, and, at its best, it merely served to 'interiorize' and 'complete' its object, substituting one naturalization – of *Homo economicus* in Smith and Ricardo – for another.[88] In this way, Marx's theories are 'taken in by the [same] socially produced appearance (*Schein*)' of economic objectivity that Marx's critique itself attempted to decipher.[89] In taking for granted the appearance of value as having been 'created' by a substantial, physical, concrete brand of labour, Marx adopted a part of the object he sought to critique, namely Ricardo's labour theory of value. Since then, over the course of its reception, 'Marx's theory of value has been mistakenly identified with the classical, or Ricardian, labour theory of value', and not, as we will go on to see, the study of 'the specific social form of labour' that we find elsewhere in Marx.[90] Part of the difficulty arises from the fact 'that Marx left behind no finished version of the labour theory of value'. In this context, 'there remains ... an urgent priority ... to reconstruct out of the more or less fragmentary presentations and the numerous individual remarks strewn in other works, the whole of the value theory'.[91] Rather than a question of theological correctness, uncovering the essence of Marx's work is more a matter of where to place emphasis in his sprawling and unfinished output. Stressing the 'labour' theory of value or his theory of exploitation, as we have done here alongside other 'substance' theories of value, only serves to 'neglect his originality and reduce him to something which was already reached before'.[92] As we see next, it is rather the specific *monetary* character of his theory that distinguishes it from what went before, moving closer to later 'subjective' theories of value as a relation than the 'objective' theories of value as a substance considered in this chapter. This can be done only by 'tearing the theory apart and putting it together in a new form to reach the goal that it has set itself better', in the words of Jurgen Habermas.[93]

2
Value as Relation

According to Philip Mirowski, 'field' theories of value hold that 'Things are valuable because people think they are.'[1] Where substance theories of value took inspiration from the early science of energy conservation, field theories take inspiration from the new science of energy as a relation between things 'constitutive of the field' and not intrinsic to any material property belonging to its elements – individuals, commodities and so on. Field theories redress classical political economy's tendency to 'elevate production above consumption and circulation as the true arbiter of the wealth of nations', conceptually resituating value away from its association with a substance bestowed in production to its status as a relation struck primarily 'within the mind as a field of preferences' in exchange.[2] Identifying in monetary exchange the capacity to effect the commensuration necessary to the value relation was not in itself new, and is inherent in Aristotle's pinpointing of the problem of value in the condition whereby 'there can be no exchange without equality, and no equality without commensurability'.[3] As we shall see, Marx took up both the challenge of this problematic, and the solution Aristotle proposed to it: the 'invention of money' as a general equivalent and expression of value by means of price.[4] Informed by the so-called 'new reading' of Marx encapsulated in the work of Hans-Georg Backhaus, Michael Heinrich, Helmut Reichelt and others, we see Marx develop what is by no means a labour theory of value in any real sense, but rather a distinctively *monetary* 'value theory of labour' that moves the discussion on from substance to the field of relations through which value is attributed and determined.[5] In this chapter, we explore how such a theory cohered in its modern guise, initially in the work of mercantilists and political economists who rejected value altogether, and later in the fullest development of Marx's critique of political economy in *Capital*, paving a largely untrodden path to marginalism.

The Denial of Value

As we saw in the previous chapter, eighteenth-century 'balance of trade' mercantilists sought to conserve the value substance in a national currency, contained within national borders where, they believed, it was produced and rightfully belonged. In so doing, they gave expression to the first true conservation theory of value in Western economic thought. Meanwhile, another 'free trade' strand of mercantilism saw no such zero-sum game, encouraging the development of new domestic markets for international goods as a spur to 'greater achievements, harder work, greater power, and augmented wealth'. In so doing, they not only threw out any theory of value as contained in money, but 'any value principle at all', with one 'free trade' mercantilist contending that 'things are just worth so much as they can be sold for' and 'things have no value in themselves, it is opinion and fashion [that] brings them into use and gives them value'. No theory of an underlying substance contained in any physical medium was necessary, and certainly not one that posited the nation state as its sole unit of reference. As Mirowski writes, 'if everything – the whole of social existence – may be indifferently bought and sold as commodities' – a key principle of the idea of free trade and its extension – 'where is the Archimedean point from which one might posit a value index other than money?'[6] Once the latter is done away with, the whole edifice of value itself falls with it. This had the advantage of getting past the conservation principle, implying 'no quantification and therefore no valid physical analogy' was possible.

This gave expression to a countervailing tradition in value inquiry – the position which denies the relevance of the category of value altogether, stating simply that all that is needed to understand the worth of something is the price that someone paid for it. Similarly, early political economist Samuel Bailey considered value essentially unmeasurable, and therefore not a useful category through which to understand the intercourse between humans, markets, commodities and the societies of which they are a part. Bailey described 'the relationality of value' as something neither 'positive or intrinsic, but merely the relation in which two objects stand to each other as exchangeable commodities'. Further still: 'A thing cannot be valuable in itself without reference to another thing, any more than a thing can be distant in itself without reference to another thing.'[7]

Contextualized within scientific advances of the time, Bailey's work was an early breakthrough for the application of non-Euclidean geometric principles to the understanding of value as a relationship between things. This, for Bailey, principally concerned the question of measure, and whether it was feasible to measure value in the same way that any physical quantity could be captured in number. In a critique of the conservation principles of Ricardian political economy, Bailey argued that 'it has been taken for granted that we measure value as we measure extension, or ascertain weight; and it has been consequently imagined, that to perform the operation we must possess an object of invariable value'. The idea one could measure value as one measures height falls in front of the fact that 'the very term absolute value implies the same sort of absurdity as absolute distance'. Value, in this respect, is not something contained within commodities, but is 'at best ... a pure relation'.[8] As Bailey writes:

> What then is possible to do in the way of measuring value? All that is practicable appears to be simply this: if I know the value A in relation to B, and the value of B in relation to C, I can tell the value of A and C in relation to each other and consequently their comparative power of purchasing all other commodities. This is an operation obviously bearing no resemblance at all to the measuring of length.[9]

The issue here is that, unlike the ruler used to measure length, the instrument used to measure value – money – is not invariant, but contingent and subject to the whim and fiat of states, and so on. But Bailey went further than seeing the absence of an invariant measuring rod as merely a problem confronting the expression of an underlying structure of value that remained intact but unseen. He contended that 'since there was no such thing as an economic invariant, *there is no such thing as value*', because we have no means to know it, however much money performs the temporary and practical function of a reasonably effective stopgap and placeholder.

The problem with this account, whilst superficially an effective riposte to substantialist approaches to value, is that it commits a similar error to the latter. In positing a ratio between commodities, there remained a concept of conservation, albeit with a reservation around the correct means to uncover that conserved. On Bailey's reasoning, 'why does anyone ever find it necessary to interpose a third commodity between any arbitrary pair in order to express price? If the choice of that third commodity really is arbitrary, then why is it required at all? If there really is no function for money to perform ... then why does it exist?'[10]

In suggesting 'no economic phenomenon is conserved through time, and therefore scientific analysis is impossible', and denying the viability of any and 'all calculation of consequences of all economic activity', Bailey is guilty of a kind of disabling 'nihilism'. Disavowing all but price itself, it did not seek to enquire any further beyond this 'real appearance' why it should be so that an abstract economic compulsion such as value should exert such a demonstrable pull on human actors, worker and capitalist alike. Eliding the real-world structuring effects of value upon everyday life under capitalism, it trips up on the reality that we do, day by day, trade in such calculations and consequences. Indeed, our capacity to eat and live at all is counted in them. Even if imperfect, it is money that denominates whatever it is we can call value or price in the first place – so much so that an act of exchange unmediated by it 'has no analytical implications for price or for anything else'.[11]

It is from this principle of brute reality that Marx criticizes Bailey.[12] Marx sees that one cannot free the world of value in thought without reckoning with the fact that it is a day-by-day factor in our lives, taking the appearance of money. Noting the absence of a fully worked-out concept of the work money does in establishing the grounds for exchangeability, Marx, in the third part of his *Theories of Surplus Value*, argues against Bailey's notion 'that a single act of exchange in itself reduces the goods exchanged to equivalence'. Marx argues instead that 'reduction to equivalence depends upon the general exchangeability, through the market, of every commodity with every other commodity'.[13] In this respect, an operationalizable theory of the comparison of values through time, regardless of its objective basis, is a condition for the continued reproduction of the capitalist and of society itself, and thus also of any theory of political economy designed to comprehend this process.[14]

In this way, Marx thought that Bailey had simply transferred the fetish from a reification of labour to that of pure relationality. In seeing value as nothing more than price, Bailey 'confuse[d] the form of value with value itself'.[15] In this respect, Bailey saw 'only value's *quantitative* aspect', and thus did not grasp the truly radical and outlying position within extant value inquiry at that time: that value is an abstract, qualitative social form that appears in quantity, rather than being something directly quantifiable itself.[16] It took Marx's theory to get this far, and with this insight to open up the possibility of a social theory of value, and it in part was Bailey's critique of the labour theory of value in the work of Ricardo and Smith that provoked Marx's radical 'Marxian turn' from a substantialist mode of value inquiry to a more sceptical one attuned to the value form, abstract labour and the concept of socially necessary labour time.[17] Marx took from Bailey the vital insight that, insofar as 'something has capitalist value in the very condition of being exchangeable', there is in the final analysis 'no transcendental value' and thus only 'a struggle over the terms of substance and measure, unique to each historical moment', the contesting of which 'challenge[s] the logic by which something becomes a bearer of value in capitalist society'.[18] From this insight flowed a new mode of value inquiry in Marx's later works, probably impossible without Bailey's bold denial of the concept as it had appeared up to that point in the work of the classical political economists.

Marx

As we saw in Chapter 1, within the context of an immanent critique of classical political economy, Marx's labour theory of value largely marks a continuation of 'objective' theories of value as a conserved substance.[19] However, the careful reinterpretation of Marx's written output made possible by the Marx–Engels Gesamtausgabe (MEGA), the gradually progressing collection of everything he committed to paper – if not to print – has shown that 'Marx's legacy is not a finished work, but rather a research programme, the vast outlines of which are only now becoming visible.'[20] This 'new reading of Marx' reveals a second version of the value theory that we can reconstruct from Marx's work, which is much closer to a 'subjective' theory of value, as a relation between – and not within – things arbitrated in exchange.[21] In this account, Marx's theory of value constitutes a 'value theory of labour' that starts from money and commodities in order to explain labour, and not the Ricardian 'labour theory of value' that represents the reverse.[22] Rather than a simple descendent of classical political economy, then, this value theory of labour might better be thought of also as an antecedent of neoclassical economics and the subjective theories of value on which it centres – although not without producing a radical theoretical remainder irreducible to and irreconcilable with such binaries.

The significance of this shift and the force of Marx's assault on existing theories was blunted by a residual commitment to conservation principles in how he presented value in his mature economic work. Instead of clearing his theoretical throat, Marx frequently lapsed back into physicalist imagery, and 'indiscriminately mixed both versions of the labor theory of value throughout *Capital*, using one or the other as it suited the problem at hand, as if they were effectively interchangeable'.[23] This polyvalence around the relationship between value and labour stems from a number of factors: the fragmentary and often provisional character of much of his posthumously published and repackaged output; the dialectical intricacies of how Marx described a contradictory reality whose existence is mediated in abstract forms of appearance which at times it was necessary to adopt as terms of an immanent critique; and a subservience to political conditions, not least the demands of communicating complex concepts to a workers' movement powered by a conviction of its own creative power and the injustice of the appropriation of its products by capital. Rather than an untouchable scriptural orthodoxy, then, Marx's work is open to reconstruction.

By the standards of popular and academic representations of what Marx's work means, this throws up some surprising insights. Rather than value being determined by the expenditure of concrete labour time, we see value determined by the socially necessary standard arbitrated in the buying and selling of its commodified outputs, for which the relevant social form is abstract labour mediated by means of money in exchange. This exhibited, for the first time, a 'field' understanding of value as a relation between things. At a time where, in the natural sciences, 'theories of ethers, subtle fluids and other such pervasive substances were in retreat', 'the cozy Euclidean world was being eyed speculatively by certain mathematicians', and 'alternative explanations in terms of forces and fields were gaining adherents', Marx's own shift stood at the precipice of a wider relativist turn in economic theories of value. Whilst it is true that 'no one individual can be credited with the full reconceptualization of value as a field', Marx was among the first to fall in line behind the new intellectual possibilities.[24] In advocating such a relational view of value, Marx 'violated almost every precept' that he had seemingly 'wished to champion concerning the importance of history, the primacy of production, the continuity of classical economics, the exchange of equivalents, and the inevitability of the fall of the capitalist rate of profit'.[25] At its best, then, his work represents this wider 'epistemic break between classical and neoclassical economics'.[26] Indeed, this shift in Marx's value theory repositioned him 'as a proto-Austrian', foreshadowing what would later become marginalism, rather than as 'a post-Ricardian' trailing in the wake of the classicals.[27]

Whilst classical political economists took labour and the costs of production to determine value, and discounted finance as an unproductive leech on the forces of the 'real' economy, Marx, even whilst remaining politically indebted to substantialism, took a much more 'subtle' approach that avoids some of their productivist pitfalls.[28] This is because of a crucial, key concept that stole a march on Marx's forebears, the significance of which has seldom been recognized by either his critics or his advocates.[29] This is the distinction between concrete labour – as a waged performance of labour taking place within the time and space of the production process – and abstract labour – labour in general, lacking practical existence in the production process, but brought into being in its representation in the commodity and expressed in money. The concrete labour that goes into the production of a given good or service will be characterized by specificities of skill, intensity, standardization and so on. In the exchange of commodities for money, this concrete specificity is abstracted from in the equivalence posited between products, which empties the labour that produced them of content and establishes an undifferentiated measure of homogeneous human labour, given form in money as a medium of exchange. For Marx, value was 'the result of [this] social process which validates the concrete, individual labor spent as a part of the total social labor'.[30] Thus, circulation is not a secondary moment in the relationship between value and labour, but constitutes it:

> in its concrete form, labour does not yet directly enter the social economy. Labour becomes social in a commodity economy only when it acquires the form of socially equalized labour, namely, the labour of every commodity producer becomes social only because his product is equalized with the products of all other producers [on the market, through sale]. [The] equalization of labour may take place, but only mentally and in anticipation, in the process of direct production, *before* the act of exchange. But in reality, it takes place through the act of exchange, through the equalization (even though it is mentally anticipated) of the product of the given labour with a definite sum of money.[31]

This non-substantialist way of understanding Marx's value theory appears to link value with demand in a style suggestive of the future course taken by marginal utility theory. Certainly, there is a focus on the role of exchange that seemingly sets it on such a road. There is a tendency within traditional Marxism to see use value as an opposing principle to exchange value, replete with an idealized vision of post-capitalist society as a retreat into use value pure and simple, freed of the abstraction of exchange. But use value is not some pre-existing essence over which exchange-value rules.[32] For Marx, use value and exchange value must be seen as mutually implicated appearances of the same process, whereby the latter becomes the form assumed by the first.[33] Marx's work suggests that 'it is precisely the fact that use-value can only exist in specific forms that provides the *reason* for exchange in its most basic form of one commodity for another: i.e. because use value is specific, commodities differ from each other as use-values and this provides a reason for exchanging them'.[34] Likewise, use value in turn depends upon the relationship of exchange, because, 'Something that is not useful cannot be sold: a cheese which has gone off cannot be sold. The opposite is also true – a commodity that is not sold cannot be used: unsold food is thrown into locked skips.'[35] As Marx writes, 'only the act of exchange can prove whether that labour is useful for others, and its product consequently capable of satisfying the needs of others'.[36]

Hence, monetary exchange plays a pivotal role in securing the equivalence of goods and services as commodities. Of course, there are numerous examples whereby the act of exchange does not entail commensurability, such as the exchange of Christmas gifts or household chores.[37] But Marx is not interested in simple commodity production and an ahistorical concept of exchange, but rather the expanded historically specific form it assumes in capitalist society. Indeed, examples used by Marx in his writings, such as the exchange of basic commodities like corn and iron, should be taken as an indication that exchange so described refers not to the individual act of trading corn for iron in a direct way, but rather to the 'whole process of exchange from which this one example has been abstracted'.[38] In exchange, money expresses the almost infinite interchangeability of all commodities with one another, an interchangeability from which no individual commodity can be isolated and allowed to stand on its own specific value:

> each commodity is interchangeable in definite, known proportions with thousands and thousands of other commodities whether or not it is actually exchanged with them. It is the fact that the interchangeability is independent of any one particular act of exchange, but is nevertheless the unplanned outcome of the sum total of autonomous acts of exchange, which posits capitalist exchange as exchange of equivalents. ... It is not exchanges as individual acts which posit equivalence, but interchangeability – the fact that we know the exchange-value of one commodity in terms of many other commodities even though it has not actually exchanged with any of them.[39]

Value is this relationship between all things, expressed in money. As such, the commodity is not just some useful or desirable use value, but carries, in its exchange value, a relationship to all the other commodities on the market, mediated by money and expressed in price. As such, 'outside of their relationship to each other – the relationship where they are equated', commodities do not 'contain objective value' at all.[40] Value is not an objective 'thing' that can be produced and embedded in a product, but a relation 'bestowed *mutually* in the act of exchange'.[41] A product of labour on its own, then, is neither value-bearing nor a commodity. The product of labour is only such when it enters into exchange.[42] For Marx, the commodity enters the market in its 'natural form' as a material product, but the materiality of its use value is lost as soon as it acquires an exchange value in the marketplace – its value form.[43] The chain of equivalences into which the commodity enters posits what Marx calls the 'abstract objectivity' of human labour that treads the line between a 'thing of thought' and a 'thinglike' reality in the world itself. Whilst it must reveal its thinglike materiality to be consumed, the product of labour simultaneously transforms itself 'into a fantasy' in the form it assumes as a commodity. As a commodity, the product owes nothing to any property of the natural form in which its component parts entered the world.[44] The commodity is, rather, the 'form of appearance' of the value the product of labour represents – in other words, the value form.[45]

* * * *

The concept of abstract labour and the discovery of the value form is decisive in enabling Marx to surpass the classical political economists, who posited a direct link between concrete labour and value. To the extent that Smith considers the equalization of labours at all, it was in the 'the subjective equality of the labours of individuals' struck in the exchange of commodities by their owners, independent of specific social or historical context, whereby 'Equal quantities of labour, at all times and places, may be said to be of equal value to the labourer.' But what Marx achieves with the concept of abstract labour is an account of the *objective* and not purely subjective character of this equalization of 'unequal quantities of labour forcibly brought about by the social process' of commodity exchange in capitalist society.[46]

Similarly, the development of a concept of abstract labour enables Marx to surpass the achievements of Ricardo. As we saw in the previous chapter, Marx found Ricardo's attempt to get below the surface appearance of bourgeois economic relations appealing, and in many ways carried over his labour theory of value in the exploration of the rate of exploitation and its bearing upon the production of surplus value through the division of the working day into necessary and surplus components. But the development of the concept of abstract labour reveals how Ricardo's approach is hamstrung by his focus upon the quantitative magnitude of surplus value determined by the expenditure of portions of direct physical human labour, rather than the qualitative form this labour assumes in the exchange of its production – in other words, how the valorization process mediates the results of the labour process.

Having said this, Marx himself has been subject to criticisms centring on the perception that a continued substantialism characterizes the concept of abstract labour, of which Eugene von Bohm-Bawerk's is one of the earliest and most challenging.[47] Bohm-Bawerk's criticism of Marx begins from the principle that commodities must contain and represent different types of labouring activity. As such, labour in the first instance must always assume the guise of concrete labour, the specificity and character of which grants the particular commodity its use value. Abstract labour abstracts from this concrete labour. Up to this point, Bohm-Bawerk's understanding neatly matches that we have ascribed to Marx above. But, perhaps understandably in the context of the polyvalence of *Capital* on the matter, Bohm-Bawerk misreads Marx as presenting abstract labour as something with a practical existence, rather than something conjured in the moment of exchange. It is this that makes possible what has stood the test of time as a particularly debilitating assault on the sophistication of Marx's value theory. Bohm-Bawerk paints Marx as holding that abstract labour only has concrete existence through concrete labour, a tautology that, applied across different commodities possessing different use values, renders impossible the claim that any kind of 'general' labour can be the common property of all commodities. Bohm-Bawerk suggests that the diversity of labour, such as that between skilled and unskilled labour, precludes the existence of abstract labour as a valid category.

In Bohm-Bawerk's critique, therefore, Marx's theory of value 'appears to collapse upon its own dialectical foundations'. Put simply, 'If abstract labour exists only as concrete labour ... it can have no mode of existence apart from concrete labour in all its various forms'.[48] But, in these respects, Bohm-Bawerk's critique hits its target only by attributing to Marx a belief in an eternal human labour in general that, embodied in commodities, determines their value – a position closer to Ricardo than to Marx himself. Marx's own work had already answered Bohm-Bawerk's by surpassing conceptions of embodied labour, whether concrete or abstract, for a relational one that attributed the sole responsibility for the drawing of equivalence between commodities – and thus the social mediation of abstract labour, into which the concrete labour expended in their production enters – to exchange rather than production.[49] As Marx writes, 'the reduction of various concrete private acts of labor to this abstraction of equal human labor is only carried out through exchange, which … equates products of different acts of labor with each other'.[50]

Marx and Marginalism

In this second theory of value that we find in Marx, then, substantialism is 'renounced' entirely, insofar as the past production of the commodity leaves no trace in any conserved substance.[51] Thus, Marx writes that value rests in 'the quantity of labour required to produce' the commodity not in a direct fashion dependent on a labour substance expended in production, but as a socially determined standard subject to foregoing conditions of production and exchange.[52] 'Value creation' is thus not a practical, technical process that embodies in products a conserved substance imparted by labour.[53] Rather, the notion that value is a property transferred into the product by labour is little more than an *a-posteriori* 'hallucination' that nonetheless acts as a predicate of the process of production itself.[54] In this sense, the 'hallucination' is not a mere figment of the imagination, but a 'real abstraction' produced through human activity that takes on a concrete social form in structuring the purposes and outcomes of production. A 'real abstraction' is 'not the result of analytical effort', or a subjective example of some kind of 'false consciousness', but an *a-priori* condition that is the 'consequence of a real process' in social and economic practices of exchange.[55] In other words, 'it exists nowhere other than the human mind but it does not spring from it', taking shape in the monetary expectations of value and profit invested and embedded in production from the off.[56]

Whilst value is not determined prior to exchange, then, it also does not originate, or is somehow 'produced' entirely 'coincidentally', through the exchange act itself. Whether or not the monetary expectations set at the commencement of the round of production will be met, and surplus value generated, rests on a process of social *validation* of expended labour as productive of value.[57] Rather than anything intrinsic to the labour or its exchange, it is how the latter mediates the former that is distinctive. Labour in its practical doing is private and pre-social, and it becomes social only through the exchange relation.[58] The retrospective appraisal of value creation can be applied only where individual private labours are subsequently recognized as productive parts of the total abstract labour of society through the exchange of their products for money.[59] Thus, value is a 'contingent state' that attaches itself to a commodity only where the conditions of the 'contemporary configuration of production' are met, in conformity to 'best-practice techniques' in the workplace and 'effective demand conditions' for the products of that private labour in the market.[60]

The conditions that must be satisfied in the workplace relate to the criterion of what Marx called 'socially necessary labour time' (SNLT), which differs from direct labour-time embodied in the commodity insofar as it represents the amount of labour required to produce a good or service under average conditions of production and in line with the requirements for the reproduction of that labour.[61] Unlike in classical political economy, then, for Marx value does not consist in the amount of labour-time expended in production by any one labouring individual, but in the amount of time 'socially required for its production'.[62] This abstract measure of the 'time taken' for the job is not predetermined in production itself, but set by a process of 'social averaging' achieved through the mediation of labours in the exchange of their products as commodities in the market.[63] The conformity of a given round of production with SNLT is also 'validated only by exchange in the market'.[64] Exchange establishes the extent to which it meets 'the social necessity of the labour expended for the production of a particular commodity'.[65] Marx suggests that 'If the market cannot stomach the whole quantity' of a given product 'at its normal price ... the effect is the same as if each individual weaver [or other worker] had expended more labor time on his particular product than was socially necessary'.[66] The successful sale of the products of labour confirms that the round of production has met the conditions for its validation as value-producing, having proceeded in line with prevailing standards of productivity and attracted sufficient effective demand in the marketplace. The products are thus validated as commodities possessed of exchange value, and the concrete labour that went into their production is abstracted from as part of the total social whole.[67] In this way, SNLT and the abstraction of labour are inseparable concepts in this second, relational version of Marx's value theory.

The concept of 'validity' is central here, and acts as a means by which the relationship between human conceptuality and abstract labour is articulated whilst carefully walking the line between the objective and the subjective sides of value. In early versions of *Capital*, the appendix on 'The Value Form', later integrated into the main text of the second edition, contains more than thirty mentions of validity in its various lexical derivations. Whilst situated in the wider context of Marx's continuing appeal to a substantialist conceptualization of the relationship between abstract labour and value, the treatment of validity shows a certain degree of 'desubstantialisation', a move from 'substance to subject', in the development of Marx's value theory.[68] Perhaps owing to the necessity of cleansing the text of such metaphysical subtleties for a wider audience, the references to validity are retained to a lesser degree in the second edition. Take this passage from *Capital* in its English translation: 'The total labour-power of society, which is [expressed] in the [values] of all commodities, *counts* [*gilt*: is valid] here as one homogeneous mass of human labour-power.'[69] The translation of *gilt* as *counts* is here crucial. As with so many other issues in Marx, much clarity can be gained by a return to the German in order to render transparent the theoretically deliberate choices made by translators. The translation of *gilt* as 'counts' suggests a purely quantitative and objective dimension and diminishes the claim being made. The translation of *gilt* as 'is valid' possesses a different implication altogether. This is because 'validity in its strict sense is tied to subjects, for whom something has validity – without subjects no validity'.[70] In this sense, the centrality of social validity to the determination of abstract labour – and, therefore, value – brings Marx's developed value theory into the sphere of a 'subjective' theory of value, edging towards a position whereby 'a thing's value derives from its being incorporated into a system of discriminations, rather than anything intrinsic to it'.[71]

This also implies a reconciliation with the category of price, resonating with later neoclassical theories of value. Marx's monetary theory of value is distinguished from the classicals by the insight that 'money is the necessary form of appearance of value'. The 'price-form *is* the value-form', for only in money can both the exchange value and, therefore, the use value of a commodity be granted a form of expression separate from the commodity itself.[72] Many traditional Marxists have followed in the footsteps of contemporaries of Marx such as Proudhon, who sought to separate value and price rather crudely along positive and negative lines, proposing that all would be well so long as price reflected values.[73] But, in this 'second' Marx, price is accepted as a specific and important social category itself, rather than merely an illusion to be stripped away. For Marx, value, by its very existence, is 'always and immediately trans-formed into prices', and, conversely, value is 'expressed only through the mediation of price', without which its existence 'makes no sense'.[74] Thus, rather than price being an artificial layer of mystification cloaking value production, in Marx's relational value theory, there is no other means to know value than price, the establishment of which grants value a means of expression separate from the commodity that carries it, and in so doing validates the labour that created it as a part of the total social abstract labour of society as a whole.[75] Price is not something secondary, but, by means of money as the general equivalent, makes possible the commensuration of labours on which the value relation rests. In this way, Marx suggests that 'money causes the circulation of commodities by realising their prices' and bringing them into a relationship of exchangeability and equivalence with all other things.[76] Picking up the thread of the Aristotelian position briefly mentioned at the outset of this chapter, the prefiguration of a marginalist position that holds price to express utility is plain to see.

* * * *

One of the most compelling critiques of this interpretation of Marx's value theory comes courtesy of Robert Kurz. The targets of his critique are scholars like Isaak Rubin and Michael Heinrich, who have been central in developing the 'new reading' of Marx outlined above. Approaches to Marx's value theory that stress the role of circulation rather than production in the constitution of value, Kurz suggests, commit a naturalistic fallacy, in that they posit concrete labour as a physiological expenditure logically and historically prior to the imposition of abstract labour in exchange, and thus 'ontologise' the specific form production assumes in capitalist society as something transhistorical and unchanging, with only the social form in which its results are mediated distinguishing one kind of society from another.[77] In this way, Kurz claims, 'circulationist' perspectives on Marx's value theory focus too narrowly on the conditions under which the equalization of labours and distribution of value takes place, rather than production itself. Kurz characterizes those approaches that situate abstract labour in commodity exchange as perceiving the problem with capitalism to pertain only to the juridical relations that govern the buying and selling of labour power – the sphere of 'Freedom, Equality, Property and Bentham' that Marx sought to escape – leaving production pristinely untouched.[78] This, Kurz argues, leaves it no better or wiser than productivist traditional Marxism.

The external relation the new reading of Marx presupposes, between concrete production and abstract circulation, mimics, Kurz proposes, the traditional critique of capitalism offered by 'labour movement Marxism', insofar as production is left untroubled by critique, and the problem of capitalism is instead seen to pertain to circulation alone. On this basis, he charges it with a 'naturalism of production' similar, in some sense, to that which might plausibly be levelled against productivist substance theories of value, with their suspicion of the money-form as an 'unkosher' imposition on the production of useful things.[79] The main difference, for Kurz, is that, where traditional substantialist readings of Marx posited the working class as the producer of all wealth, the value of which was then determined in circulation, the new reading of Marx removes labour and the labourer from the equation, stripping class subjectivity from the process of value creation.

Shorn of a rhetorical valorization of worker power, the new reading of Marx therefore reduces political action to the search for an extension of the bourgeois 'fair play' found in the exchange of other commodities to the buying and selling of labour power.[80] This insists on the bourgeois Enlightenment ideology of the 'universality and egalitarianism of the sphere of circulation', which takes on the guise of the 'condemnation of "injustice"' addressed through regulatory or distributive actions, and the 'invocation of the democratic ideals of freedom and equality' presupposed on a 'political subject, a legal person', defined by its status as a commodity owner – of labour power, in the case of workers. The circulationist approach to Marx's value theory therefore ironically finds itself sitting at the 'last line of defence of democratic and Enlightenment ideas' – where, one might argue, any revisionist Marxism worth its salt should be.[81]

From this persepctive, Kurz suggests that the new reading of Marx resonates with classical political economy, even whilst refuting its substantialism. Seeing the 'mode of socialisation' specific to capitalism resting solely in money and exchange, Kurz argues, shifts the terrain of the social to the sphere of circulation in much the same way as suggested in the bourgeois Enlightenment ideology of Smith and others, which defined humans by their 'propensity to truck, barter and exchange'. According to this account, Kurz suggests, history would comprise nothing more than changing modes of 'exchange' and 'circulation', rather than production, with differences in the otherwise '"eternal" purely natural production' relegated in significance as merely 'technical' tweaks on the ultimately unchanging natural order of things.[82]

This lapse into 'bourgeois basal ideology', Kurz contends, lights the passage of anti-substantialist, relational readings of Marx's value theory into the subjective theories of value associated with marginalism.[83] The theoretical priority granted to circulation in the concept of the 'exchange abstraction' breaks with any concept of substance underpinning value theory, in precisely the same way, Kurz suggests, as 'the subjective value theory of bourgeois economics'.[84] There is something in this, as we have seen. However, as we will

go on to see, what distinguishes the new reading of Marx
from a purely subjective 'bourgeois' economics of 'psychical
processes' such as 'utility estimations' and 'preferences' is the
social *objectivity* that value, as a real abstraction, attains as
a form of mediation between things.[85] As we shall see in the
next chapter, whilst it is undoubtedly true that the second
'relational' Marx presented here set in train a 'field' theory
of value that was taken forward by marginal utility theory,
and that there persist vital commonalities between Marx's
developed value theory and marginalism, there are also
fundamental differences.

* * * *

Indeed, contrary to Kurz's assertion that the new reading
of Marx ideologically preserves the Eurocentric ontological
and epistemological privilege of the 'white Western male
subject' and its Enlightenment project, the new reading's
relational understanding of Marx's value theory has been
used to underpin cutting-edge confrontations with structures of racial domination and discrimination.[86] A recurring
concern uniting Kurz and scholars associated with the new
reading of Marx is comprehending and combating the
theoretical foundations of antisemitism, specifically in its
left-wing or pseudo-anticapitalist variant.[87] With reference
to the fetishistic appearances assumed by capitalist social
forms, this literature has sought to critically explain some
kinds of left and right antisemitism as foreshortened or
truncated attempts to articulate critiques of the abstract
character of social domination in a world ruled by the
value form. The literature suggests that, seeking concrete
agents to hold responsible for an agentless system of social
domination, conspiracist critiques of capitalism incorrectly
and dangerously personify abstract wealth in the individual
and collective figure of the Jew, whether directly or indirectly
through association with other guilty parties like specific
states, bankers or financial institutions.[88]

In a brilliant recent example of the capacity of this literature to confront rather than reproduce capitalist structures
of racial domination, Hylton White expands this analysis of

the relationship between fetish forms and antisemitism to
address anti-black racism, drawing from the work of Moishe
Postone and Frantz Fanon.[89] White relates the antisemitic
personification of capital in the figure of the Jew to the racist
association of blackness with 'a feral bodily power that can
be socialised only by taming it', a 'brute biological force that
lacks self-governing will and is thus in need of socialising
violence to make it useful to civil society'. Depicted by turns
as both 'potent' and 'recalcitrant', this 'essentially biological
body' can be deployed as a 'force of production' only when
'harnessed with dominating power'. In this, anti-blackness
personifies in the black body abstract labour as a 'social
force abstracted from individual or wilful action', a 'visceral
human capacity' – in other words, how abstract labour in
general appears in the mystified fetish form it assumes in
capitalist society. This personification is the dialectical mirror
image of how, owing to a precapitalist legacy of anti-Jewish
racism centring on 'the identification of Jews with commerce
and usury', some forms of antisemitism personify in the
figure of the Jew abstract wealth or 'dematerialised value'.[90]

In this way, White argues, 'the ideological pair of antisemitism and antiblack racism gives us human proxies for these
fetish forms' – abstract labour and abstract value – 'casting
the pathologies of modernity not as the outcome of a
structure of alienation, but as the powers of antisocial racial
types'.[91] The difference is that the force of monetary value
personified in the Jew is 'a power of control', whereas the
force of the abstract biological capacity personified in the
black of antiblack racism is 'a power that requires control'.[92]
This plays out in the practical form these racisms assume.
As Fanon notes, where antisemitism associates Jewishness
with an intellectual and abstract wealth or will to power of
a whole race, which is persecuted on this totalizing basis,
the bodily power of black racialized subjects is dominated
in its specific concrete 'corporeality'.[93] Antisemitism is the
'paranoid fear of a people engaged in conspiracies of will'
guided by an 'invisible, untraceable intelligence', the racist
imaginary of which invites a violence that seeks to 'flush
out and destroy an entire people, as a people'. Blackness,
meanwhile, is associated by antiblack racism not with control
but with its precise opposite – 'an uncontrolled bodily

energy' that is dominated and destroyed not in the search for and prosecution of a whole race but in its individual 'concrete, corporeal, visible' instantiations. For Fanon, 'this is the key generic difference between the industrialised mass murder of the Holocaust and the ritualised destruction of the individual black body by a lynching mob'. In both cases, a concrete culprit for abstract forms is identified, located and either destroyed or dominated. Moreover, each carries its own 'dangerously misleading form of emancipatory fantasy': antisemitism as resistance against a 'fetishistic representation of capital', and antiblackness against abstract labour as an expression of human unfreedom under capitalism.[94]

Like the association of Jewishness with valorization, antiblackness thus expresses 'an opposition generated repeatedly within the forms of capitalist society', wherein human practice as a matter of structural necessity produces 'fetishistic representations of its own functioning' that feed upon and reproduce existing prejudices in a new form. This is because 'the valorisation of capital is the outcome of an extraordinarily complex social process, and that complex social process unfolds in a way that obscures its social conditions'.[95] As we shall see in chapter 5, other Marxian approaches have accompanied the new reading of Marx to dig down deeper into the social conditions obscured behind the fetish forms of a society ruled by the abstract force of value. This is necessary work as the world continues to reckon with the causes and consequences of its constitution in and through fetishism.

3

Value as Utility

After Marx, it was neoclassical economics, and specifically utility theory, that, notwithstanding its own flaws, followed through in a more full-throated way on the promise of field theories of value. Where the reconceptualization of value as a relation is something that must be reconstructed from Marx's critique of political economy, utility is characterized by a bold and open attack on the idea of value as an 'intrinsic embodied substance'. Like Marx, it portrays value as subject to a series of 'potentials' the commodity passes through in its production and circulation, rather than as a property of the product inevitably carried through to exchange.[1] In this respect, the insights of marginalism were stimulated by the relativism afforded by advances in physics towards an understanding of energy as operating as a field, just as theories of substance were stimulated by earlier and less sophisticated scientific conceptualizations of energy as something conserved.

Moreover, just as with other theories, the rise of marginalism was informed by the political context in which it developed. Against a nationalist and protectionist position on trade influenced by substantialist theories of value, trade was reconceptualized in neoclassical economics as central to value not in its limitation between national borders, but in its extension in the name of maximization of opportunities for utility. In the 'field' of value, trade represented 'motion', enlarging the field of value through increasing the perceived utility individuals can gain from a good or marginal increases in the amount of a good.[2]

For utility theory, the heterogeneity of an 'objective' use value akin to 'the tensile strength of steel' or 'the pliability of cotton' implied the impossibility of ascribing a common material substance to value.[3] Marginalists such as William Stanley Jevons, Carl Menger and Leon Walras identified three deficiencies with the Ricardian labour theory of value inherent to much political economy up to that point.[4] The first was that any commodity with a fixed and finite supply, such as rare statues or artworks, would attract a value out of all proportion with the specific labour exerted in its production. The second was that the labour expended in the production of a commodity for which the potential demand turned out to be overestimated would not result in any realized 'value' to speak of. The third was that labour itself is heterogeneous, and the only means through which it can be compared in the final instance is by means of the exchange of its products – exposing a circularity that undermines the attempt of Ricardo and others to extrapolate the value of products from labour.

This led instead to an explanation of value rooted in 'the *subjective* properties of these self-same objective characteristics', centred on the 'utility' perceived to be gained from them in different quantities.[5] In so doing, 'The new neoclassical school of economic theory … displaced the weight of commensurability from external substances to the mind', with the mind conceptualized, in line with the advances in physics, 'as a field of force in an independently constituted commodity space'.[6] Commodities, therefore, did not carry value within them but, rather, the latter was constituted relationally in the interchange between them on the terrain of subjective desire.

Marginal utility theory thus purports to break with substantialist value theories based on conservation principles. As a consequence, rather than drawing a productivist divide between productive and unproductive activities based on a substantialist understanding of labour inserted – as if by osmosis – into the commodity, marginalism and its theory of marginal utility refrain from moral judgement and 'states that all income is reward for a productive undertaking', insofar as what sells has value.[7] The corollary of this is also that prices represent all there is to know about the value of a good, expressing the balance of supply and of demand for a good in the context of conditions of scarcity. Price is thus 'a direct measure of value', rather than something potentially divergent or obsfucatory. The relativity of value made possible by price in the model of marginal utility renders impossible absolute measures of concrete labour and its productive contribution to value creation.[8]

But the extent to which utility theory achieves this decisive break with conservation principles is open to question. Exploring its foundations and key thinkers, this chapter will begin from utility theory's apparent break from substantialism, before exploring the extent to which, by positing a quantity common to all commodities, the util functions as a similarly substantialist principle to that espoused in classical labour theories of value.

Foundations

Whilst marginal utility theory carries over aspects of Marx's monetary 'value theory of labour' to pose a radical alternative to the labour theories of value that dominated classical political economy, it does partake in common problematics running through modern value theory. Most significantly among these continuing preoccupations, the theory of marginal utility helps to ground conceptually the paradox of how use value and exchange value diverge, which was uncovered by Adam Smith: 'Nothing is more useful than water: but it will purchase scarce any thing; scarce any thing can be had in exchange for it. A diamond, on the contrary, has scarce any value in use; but a very great quantity of other goods may frequently be had in exchange for it.'[9] For the lack of a theory of utility, Smith left this paradox largely unexplained.[10] Ricardo made further work of it, establishing of this paradox that 'Value in use cannot be measured by any known standard; it is differently estimated by different persons' in the price they are willing to pay.[11] Later, the marginalist Alfred Marshall would read into Ricardo's presentation the presence of a notion of limited supply reducing total utility and increasing the marginal utility of a good, although there is scant basis for such a reading.[12]

Overall, however, in the classical political economists, the theory was not quite in place to explain the paradox of value on the terms marginal utility would later attempt. But in the focus on demand as an important element of value, Smith and Ricardo made a vital contribution to the development of marginalism, in combination with insights gleaned from the utilitarian philosophy.

In its development, marginal utility theory drew upon the earlier work of Daniel Bernoulli, who, contending that evaluations of worth circulated around the expected degree of utility an individual could gain from a given thing, defined the law of diminishing marginal utility from which marginalism came to take its name.[13] Focusing on dilemmas faced by gamblers, Bernoulli suggested that small upwards variations in winnings reduced their marginal utility and thus the amount one might wager in their pursuit. This could be applied across to the amount one should be prepared to pay, for instance, for insurance against certain risks. However, there was no evidence given for the existence of either the 'utility' on which this rested or the curve it was taken to operate along. As such, other theorists of similar issues writing around the same period, such as Cournot, rested their assumptions within market appraisals – or 'demand functions' – rather than any quantity subsisting behind price.[14] This is a divergence of focus that recurs across the literature on this topic, as we shall see. Between what Stigler calls 'demand theory' and utility theory, the latter posits utility as a measurable force behind the appearances of market price, discernible in the artificial settings of an experimental method, and some among adherents of the former suggest that actual market behaviour is the best way to ascertain the value or utility placed upon something by means of the price paid, rather than the price a participant expresses a willingness to pay in abstraction from the moment of exchange itself.

Either way, Bernoulli's theorem was structural to the development of marginal utility theory. Marshall, for instance, extrapolated the theorem to the much wider potential field of socially grounded analysis that marginalism, by focusing on value as something relative as opposed to absolute, displays an often unfulfilled capacity to open out upon. For instance, Marshall considers how class position would impact upon the 'increment of happiness measured by a given sum of money' for different actors possessed of different amounts of wealth.[15] In this wider application, marginal utility took inspiration from the utilitarian calculus of pure pleasure and pain through which, in the nineteenth century, Jeremy Bentham equated the value of, for example, push-pin with that of music and poetry.[16] The quantification of the relative amounts of pleasure and pain represented in the push-pin and the poem, for Bentham, revolved around four dimensions experienced at the individual level: intensity, duration, certainty and propinquity. Whereas the first two were taken to measure pleasure directly, the latter two were taken to influence the individual response to a given pleasure. Bentham set out the social and human character circumscribing the exact dimensions of this 'sensibility', depending on 'no less than thirty-two circumstances (such as age, sex, education and firmness of mind) that must be taken into account in carrying out such a calculation'.[17]

In common with much subsequent theory in the tradition, Bentham withdrew from the interesting methodological issues this raised. 'Differences of character are inscrutable', Bentham wrote, 'and such is the diversity of circumstances', that the 'sensibility' around which assessments of utility may be made 'are never the same for two individuals'. But this qualitative heterogeneity did not prevent the making of propositions around the utility of a given good. Indeed, the making of propositions and policy around utility retrospectively justifies its methodological ascription, on the basis that they 'approach nearer the truth than any others which can be substituted for them' and 'can be made the basis of legislation'.[18] This rests on some faulty thinking, insofar as its 'interpersonal comparisons' were little more than 'question-begging' assumptions justified by their expected results, with no scientific evidence base, save for the fact that the perspective represented a convenient alibi for the production of social policy at a given point in space and time.[19] Indeed, this issue is woven within the theory, a crude empiricism around people's stated or revealed preferences taken to be sufficient to explain the theoretical principle that lies behind them, without reference to social relations and so on.

For reasons good and bad, then, Bentham was central to the development of the theory of diminishing utility – specifically, for example, in the statement that 'the quantity of happiness produced by a particle of wealth (each particle being of the same magnitude) will be less and less at every particle'.[20] And, moreover, Bentham promoted the possibilities of a leap beyond substantialist theories of value that sought a secret substance behind the social appearance of value by rooting the expression of utility solely in price, in that 'we may measure pleasures through the prices they command', and through this relate one pleasure to another.[21] That said, the placing of an emphasis on price as the expression of utility is by no means a constant in the development of the theory, however. Jules Depuit, an adherent of the nascent theory in the mid nineteenth century, posed precisely the opposite relationship, in that 'utility of any product is at a maximum when the toll or the price is zero'.[22] But, in general, the trend was towards an understanding of utility as something positively and not negatively expressed in and through price. Bentham, in his persistently stated belief that 'money was the best measure of pleasure or pain', sums this position up.[23]

The question remains as to why it was necessary to compose the 'baroque taxonomies' of which utility theory consists if money already provides an accurate basis for the understanding of pleasure. Where money is posited as a simple and unmediated reflection of value, a theory of value becomes almost redundant, in spite of the apparent statements of its proponents otherwise. This leads proponents to fill their theoretical imaginary with other elements, such as the 'moral arithmetic' which, for Bentham, was 'merely a convenient fiction and a didactic artifice' with no relationship to any real 'value theory' in the sense of seeking the conditions of commensurability between things.[24] This highlights how inherent within post-substantialist approaches to value that reject conservation principles is a tendency towards a 'denial of value' along the lines of that put forward by Bailey, with which we might also associate the monetary 'value theory of labour' espoused in Marx. In its most empiricist mode, utility theory accepts wholesale the appearances of value in money or stated and revealed preferences, rendering redundant any underpinning value theory capable of explaining how the different levels relate. It was Jevons, after all, who proposed that 'the word value ... merely expresses the circumstance of [a commodity] exchanging in a certain ratio for some other substance ... Value will be expressed, like angular magnitude and other ratios in general, by abstract number.'[25] Vowing to 'discontinue the use of the word altogether', Jevons set in motion a deep ambivalence about value inquiry itself that carries through to classics such as Gérard Debreu's *The Theory of Value*, which, as Mirowski amusingly notes, contains nary a word on its titular topic, speaking largely only of price.[26]

The Util

Even though utility theory inaugurates the neoclassical break with political economy in favour of a narrower, more scientistic 'economics', it nonetheless carries roots in classical political economy. Jean-Baptiste Say was among the first contemporaries and critics of the classicals to formulate explicitly something akin to what we now know as utility theory. Say contended that 'the value of a commodity resides in its utility to a buyer and, therefore, that productive labour is labour which produces utility'.[27] To this extent, Say was not as hung up on constructing boundaries around productive and unproductive activities as some of his contemporaries. Indeed, for Say, it did not matter what the specific content of the production process or the commodity produced actually was, whether good or service. So long as it fetched a price, and the labour that went into its production was waged, the labour that went into its production was retrospectively validated as productive – insofar as it produces utility, inspiring and consummating a desire – and the good or service as value-bearing – similar, language aside, to the relational reading of Marx's value theory presented in the previous chapter, with its underpinning notion of 'validity'. As Edmund Wilson writes, touching upon this similarity:

> If all value is created by labor only in some metaphysical sense, then there may be more in those utility theories of

value which Marxists regard as capitalist frauds than we had formerly been willing to admit. If it is possible for values to be reckoned as Marx reckoned them, in units of abstract labor power, why was it not possible – as Marx had denied – to reckon them in units of abstract utility? – especially when the supposed value of labor seems to have nothing to do with fixing prices, whereas the demand of the consumer obviously has.[28]

Following Say, Hermann Gossen was the 'first writer to formulate explicitly' what he sees as the 'fundamental principle of marginal utility theory', namely that 'A person maximises his utility when he distributes his available money among the various goods so that he obtains the same amount of satisfaction from the last unit of money spent upon each commodity'.[29] Mirowski places him at the same hinge point of the procession from classical to neoclassical economics as Hermann von Helmholtz occupied in changes in the natural sciences, around which, as in the continuing preoccupation of physics in Helmholtz's time with 'confusions over whether force or energy were substances', confusions still reigned 'over whether utility could be treated as a substance'.[30] Gossen's theory of value is a 'curious hybrid' that carries within it the 'transition in physical theory' between substance and field, and as such is neither fish nor fowl, half labour theory of value and half 'a theory of subjective psychological value'. In identifying the varying perception of utility through temporal consumption of goods, Gossen posited 'a functional relationship between what he called the pleasure of experiences and the time duration during which the pleasure was experienced'. Utility here is not 'a variable of state', a character of the thing itself, but fully within the relational field of subjective mind. In this, Gossen went further than others had gone up until that point. Gossen 'makes much of the dictum that there exists no absolute value', an observation we earlier discussed in terms of the 'denial of value' found in such radical outliers as Samuel Bailey.[31] Moreover, he stressed 'the primacy of exchange over production', suggesting that 'the act of exchange can actually create or augment value', rather than the latter remaining unchanged as a property conserved from creation through to consumption.[32] The major real-world implication of this downgrading of production was to emphasize the importance of trade instead, which itself increased pleasure by moving goods around and opening up the opportunities for their consumption. Production would only really matter insofar as it produced novel goods that opened up avenues for trade.[33]

In this way, early utility theory was characterized by the open realization – which one must largely read between the lines in Marx's *Capital* – that labour 'does not impart a "substance" to commodities in any physical sense'.[34] Utility theorists saw it as 'impossible to compare a priori the productive powers of a navvy, a carpenter, an iron-puddler, a schoolmaster, and a barrister', and as such the value of labour cannot be the objective basis on which to ascribe value to its product.[35] Rather, the reverse is the case, and the value ascribed to the product in its exchange retrospectively validates the labour as productive of value, as in Marx. However, this break with conservation principles was left incomplete, with marginal utility theory subject to its own residual substantialism. Gossen hinted at this when he pondered whether, 'if the conserved quantity does not reside in the object, then perhaps it resides in the beholder'.[36] In neoclassical economics, this conserved substance was coined the 'util'.[37] Irving Fisher's procedure for reaching this substance was as follows:

> Select arbitrarily a quantity of any commodity, say, 100 loaves of bread. Let the marginal utility of this quantity of commodity be the unit of utility (or util). Grant the ability of the individual to order the utilities of specified amounts of two goods, i.e., to indicate a preference (if one exists) or indifference between the two quantities. Then it is possible to construct the utility schedule of (say) milk.[38]

Hence, Fisher inaugurates the concept of the util by abstracting from the appearances of the price one pays for something to posit a deeper structure, rooted in the existence of a mysterious substance just as dubious in character as the labour value that classical and Marxian substantialism thought was congealed in the commodity.[39] What conceptually differentiates the util from previous guises of a value substance may well be its relativity.[40] Fisher related the choice of the util as a unit to the social relation between people and their capacity to consume, suggesting that 'one's pleasure from diamonds is reduced if many other people have them (or if none do!), and one's pleasure from a given income is reduced if others' incomes rise'.[41] However, this was seldom linked into an analysis of the social field in which such demarcations and divisions are forged. As Mirowski asserts, there is seldom a variational principle without the underpinning presumption of a conservation principle to accompany it, and in this way the potential for a fully relative, field-oriented theory of value was undermined by utility theory's dependence on an order-bestowing substance to lend operationalizability to its analytical model.[42]

This is clear in the tendency among early neoclassicals to present utility functions as belonging to individual commodities.[43] Elsewhere, Fisher posits value as a kind of conserved substance hosted in the body of money.[44] However, utility, by the letter of a field theory of value, would not consist in any commodity individually, but only in the relation posited between commodities. Moreover, one of the things that sets Marx apart as a glimpse of a possible future is his conceptualization of money as a form of mediation that value must assume in order to take on an existence; but at no point does this, at the extent of its sophistication in *Capital*, imply the conservation of value *within* money. In these respects, marginalism actually takes a step back from where Marx touched down with the full development of his value theory.

Measure

The util as a unit may posit pleasure as a substance conserved in the mind of a single person, then, but to what extent is it 'comparable between minds' as an independent force capable of its own forms of expression and measure?[45] Few neoclassicals made Benthamite claims as to the quantitative comparability of the pleasure derived from push-pin and that from poetry.[46] But the apparent unquantifiability of their unit analysis did not prevent later neoclassicals from developing a science based on the relative measure of the 'utils' contained in diverse goods and services.

Attempts to measure utility took succour from the Weber–Fechner law, first developed in the 1860s.[47] This built on Bernoulli's original statement of the central principle of marginal utility theory with the research of its two psychologist progenitors. Fechner, the founder of so-called 'psychophysics', was preoccupied with the psychological effects of changes in physical elements – or, more simply, 'the relation of mind and matter'. What appealed so much to those seeking a theory of marginal utility was Fechner's concern with the situation whereby 'on one side there is a physical quantity that can vary, such as the energy of a light, the frequency of a tone, or an amount of money' and 'on the other side there is a subjective experience of brightness, pitch, or value'.[48] Meanwhile, Weber would conduct experiments along similar lines, blindfolding participants who were then handed ever-heavier amounts of weights and asked to indicate when they felt an increase. Weber found that participants sensed added weight proportional not to the absolute increase but the relative increase, such that if the weight the participant held was doubled, so would the threshold for noticing the difference. For those already holding a large weight, a large weight would be required to create a perceptible difference; for those with a small weight, an additional small weight would suffice.[49]

'Mysteriously', writes Daniel Kahneman, their inquiries found that 'variations of the physical quantity cause variations in the intensity or quality of the subjective experience'.[50] Moreover, this finding was not just limited to physical characteristics such as weight, but to 'perceptions of visions and sounds' as well.[51] The project was therefore to understand the 'psychophysical laws that relate the subjective quantity in the observer's mind to the objective quantity in the material world'.[52] Resonating with Bernoulli's theorem a century after it was first set out, this suggested that the subjective effect of an objective change was logarithmic, its intensity varying according to the proportion by which it differs from the initial amount.

Economists took from the Weber–Fechner law the comfort that it 'provided a scientific psychological foundation for the then-developing law of diminishing marginal utility', such that, just as with physical relationships like weight, 'changes in income at high levels of income would be less perceptible than changes in income at low levels of income'.[53] Politically, the evidential basis it provided was seized upon enthusiastically among reformists who saw, in the law of diminishing utility, a means by which Benthamite utilitarianism could be justified in the shape of a progressive income tax. Indeed, Jevons was pivotal to a Fabian socialist agenda that sought to reverse the influence of Marxism on the labour movement and its institutions, by arguing instead that value was dependent on demand, and 'any commodity is determined by the degree of its utility to the persons to whom it is available', in turn determining the value of the labour that produced it, rather than the latter determining value as in the theoretical imaginaries of their ideological foes on the social democratic left.[54]

* * * *

The Weber–Fechner law seemed to have overcome the issues of measuring utility, placing the theory on a stable scientific footing that could then have a real-world impact on the decisions made by policymakers and political reformers. As Francis Edgeworth contended, whilst 'atoms of pleasure … are not easy to distinguish and discern', the new law showed the possibility of observing that 'there is here a greater, there a less, multitude of pleasure units, mass of happiness'. That, he considered, was 'enough' to verify the theory.[55]

This concern with the blunt facts of everyday experience is a recurring theme in debates around the tenability of utility as a measure of value, with 'the recollection which every one must have of his own economic actions and behaviour' a sufficient basis on which to construct some impression of utility theory's veracity as a description of actual economic practice.[56] Edgeworth took this furthest with his invention of a 'hedonimeter' capable of quantifying pure pleasure in practice. Edgeworth drew upon the Weber–Fechner law to suggest that 'physio-psychology' – the 'psychophysics' of Weber–Fechner – would permit the development of tools to ascertain the 'physiological underpinning of utility' in such a way as to render the latter 'directly measurable'.[57] The hedonimeter was the result.

Fisher, the inventor of the util, took a quite different tack in the same search for measure. Whilst he was concerned with the rigorous and scientific measurement of utility, he contended that it was not possible to do this using physiological measurements that sought a *direct* measure, but only by means of an 'indirect approach that worked backwards from individual choices to measures of utility', a 'backward induction from observed behaviour to measured utility'. Fisher 'argued that economics does not need a psychophysical foundation for utility' because 'individuals reveal their utility through their actions' – in other words, what is not immediately apparent can be known through its effect.[58] This is because, contrary to the 'foisting of Psychology on Economics', as Fisher put it, there is a 'simple psychoeconomic postulate' at play that psychophysics misses: 'Each individual acts as he desires', and it is from these actions that we can measure that which lies behind them.[59]

This standpoint was informed by philosophical pragmatism, insofar as it was guided by the intuition that, 'in actual practical human life, we do proceed on just such assumptions' as those of value and utility, and, in the face of academic doubt, 'the problems of life cannot, and do not, wait'.[60] It was this devil-may-care empiricism, solving the issue of value's non-empirical reality with reference to the concrete effects it takes in the day-to-day, that won out in subsequent neoclassical graspings at the measurement of the util. But this erred towards either a kind of analytical nihilism whereby all attachment to any underlying principle was disavowed, or else a methodological weakness in inducting backwards from observed choices without regard for the context and framing of decisions by social and personal factors outside the bounds of accepted economic rationality.

* * * *

Attempts to measure utility continued apace with the development and popularization of marginalist economics.

As Stigler asserts, utility theory broke through into 'generally accepted economics' in the 1870s, with the work of Jevons, Menger and Walras. With this came a different approach to the question of value's measurability that drew more directly on the field metaphor derived from contemporary physics. Jevons was one of the first to make explicit the relationship of neoclassical economics with the burgeoning field theory in natural sciences.[61] Jevons wrote that 'the notion of value is to our science what that of energy is to mechanics', comparing utility – as an 'attraction between a wanting being and what is wanted' – to gravity, insofar as the latter related bodies occupying different 'positions and distances' in the energy field.[62]

This scientific analogy implied that the 'force' at play could also be measured, on the basis of the everyday fact that, although a 'unit of pleasure or pain is *difficult even to conceive*', it is nonetheless 'the amount of these feelings' which provokes us to 'buying and selling, borrowing and lending, labouring and resting, producing and consuming' to begin with. It is possible to quantify these feelings in the solely comparative degree to which such feelings are present, Jevons contended.[63] This enabled Jevons simultaneously to deny the measurability of utility as the substance of value, whilst 'devising a way to measure utility', nonetheless, by means of the 'familiar measuring rod of money'.[64] In this way, the util itself could not be captured but the *effect* of it could, in its relation with other effects. At stake was not a measure of the absolute pleasure gained from the purchase of a commodity, but rather the relative pleasure to be gained from one quantity of the commodity over another, expressed in its price in money.[65]

The difficulty that confronts marginalist theories of value, just as with relational Marxian theories of value, is that the substance of value each posits – whether abstract labour or the util – 'cannot be observed directly with our senses, and they cannot be examined indirectly through intermediation'. Indeed, the 'quantity' of these substances present in any given thing 'cannot be calculated, even theoretically'.[66] In common with Marx's non-empirical concept of 'abstract labour', therefore, the util was brought into focus through its *effect* in exchange, expressed in its measure by money. In researching value, we have only its surface appearances on which to rest our speculations. Absolute immeasurability poses no problem to the study of a non-empirical category such as 'marginal utility' because we can know all we need to from the effective measure of its relationality in monetary price alone.[67] One issue, of course, is that we may know 'the price of capital in dollars and cents', but not 'how many utils or hours of abstract labour this value supposedly represents'.[68] But, at their best, such a search for an underlying substance is largely abandoned in both Marxian and marginalist value theories, each having accepted the real forms of appearance through which value is knowable instead.

In marginalism, this acceptance of appearance resulted in a methodological focus on what Paul Samuelson coined 'revealed preferences', examining human choices – the 'quantitative effects of the feelings' as Jevons would put it – and inferring from them the relative utilities these choices expressed.[69] As Joan Robinson asserts, this can result in a circularity whereby '*utility* is the quantity in commodities that makes individuals want to buy them, and the fact that individuals want to buy commodities shows that they have *utility*'.[70] But marginalists broke this circularity by paying heed only to price as the expression of the mysterious util some early theorists had sought as the substance of value. As Marshall wrote, 'desires cannot be measured directly, but only indirectly, by the outward phenomena to which they give rise'.[71] Indeed, 'economics', for Marshall, is 'chiefly concerned' with this measure: the price – whether in the form of money or the commensurate amount of labour or another commodity – 'which a person is willing to pay for the fulfilment or satisfaction of his desire', such that, 'if at any time he is willing to pay a shilling, but no more, to obtain one gratification; and sixpence, but no more, to obtain another; then the utility of the first to him is measured by a shilling, that of the second by sixpence; and the utility of the first is exactly double that of the second'. [72]

Similarly, Vilfredo Pareto addressed the 'problem' of utility by means of an argument for observation and experience, rather than the supposition of theoretical quantities consisting behind appearances. In a critique of Edgeworth's attempt to measure utility, Pareto suggested that it simply did not matter whether utility was 'numeri-cally measurable' through any physical or metaphysical category or quantity – any effective theory of utility should pay heed only to 'the fact of experience', reading off from people's behaviour a transparent report of their prefer-ences based on a 'rank ordering of greater or less'.[73] Along similar lines, Gustav Cassel contended that utility required a unit of measure 'that no one could define', and instead suggested that 'one can employ demand functions directly', without recourse to 'a utility substructure' acting as a 'metaphysical entity' methodologically underlying all surface appearances.[74] Indeed, for Cassel, 'utility theory added no information on the nature of [demand] functions', as they appear in observable market behaviour. Price, paid in concrete market situations, is thus the sole means by which preference, and thus value, is represented, and not the hypothetical abstraction of utility.

A welcome attribute of this focus on demand over utility is that, where the latter has an image of a rationally calculating sovereign agent hardwired into it, demand is able to accommodate how the actual behaviour of humans often defies any attempt to ascribe a rational basis to the decisions they make. This was a preserve of the psycho-logical and pragmatist critique of utility theory from early days onwards, rejecting the simplistic appeal to utilitarian and hedonic criteria of pleasure and pain as the basis on which we can assess the choices and valuations made by human actors in the world – as William James asked, for instance, 'who smiles for the pleasure of smiling, or frowns for the pleasure of the frown? Who blushes to avoid the discomfort of not blushing?'[75] Utility theory's underrepre-sentation of irrational drives and urges later constituted a vital arm of the critiques, by Daniel Kahneman and his collaborators as well as others, of the methodological opera-tionalizing of utility in the so-called 'contingent valuation method' used by governments and businesses to ascertain the worth placed upon goods, services and resources by consumers and citizens.[76]

* * * *

The protection of the smooth surface appearance of valuation from any psychological factors is just one issue with utility theory. Political questions, social pressures, material inequality and power relations also go unrecognized in the perfect models of human rationality the theory relies on. The empirical privileging of price – whether by means of observed activity or stated preferences – leaves out the quality that lurks behind quantity, concealing political and philosophical questions about what things and principles are worth. This is made clear in national accounts where the value of weapons is added to that of medicine, for instance, presenting the one as commensurate with and equivalent to the other.[77] Neoclassical utility theory rests on the notion that, 'in perfectly competitive equilibrium, one dollar's worth of the former improves our lives just as much as one dollar's worth of the latter', for the sole and simple reason that, by virtue of having been bought and sold, they each carry a price that reveals the preference each attracts. But the conditions of equilibrium this equivalence implies are not to be found in reality. Where it is supposed, such as in the experimental method by which measures of 'contingent valuation' are taken, the hypothetical consumers are granted no say as to whether some things defy or lie beyond price. Everything has its value – utility – denominated in pounds or dollars, without dwelling on whether that thing should have been produced in the first place.

The struggle to bring measure to utility was given up in the 1930s, as considerations of issues such as contentment and happiness were increasingly deemed outside the remits of economics as a nascent 'science'.[78] Interestingly, the sociologist Max Weber played a pivotal role in this break, penning a comprehensive dismissal of the Weber–Fechner law.[79] Weber's headline contribution was that marginal utility theory 'had nothing to do with psychological principles' such as the Weber–Fechner law.[80] But also implicit within Weber's noted treatment was a critique of marginal utility as it had also appeared in the work of Bernoulli and others.[81] Firstly, he argued, the logarithmic law of diminishing marginal utility would not hold in all cases, such as luxury or illicit items. Secondly, the law works from an assumption that value concerns 'psychical reactions to external stimuli', rather than the true object of economics, which is 'observable behaviour in response to subjective needs'. Thirdly, it overlooks that economics already functions perfectly well – on its own terms at least – by working with the premise that 'man has limited means to satisfy competing ends and can allocate these means rationally to maximize the fulfilment of the ends', however much critical scrutiny Weber meted out to the 'iron cage' of rationality elsewhere in his work.[82]

Whilst Weber, on the one hand, posited that marginal utility theory could stand on its own two feet without the support of psychological principles, on the other, he made the more important claim that marginalism and the 'rational economic behaviour' it describes are 'bound up with definite social, historical, and cultural conditions ... associated with our modern capitalist society'.[83] As such, 'rational economic behaviour' could not be associated with the kind of *Homo oeconomicus* described by psychological or biological under-standings that ascribe to humans an innate 'propensity to truck, barter and exchange', for instance, or the possession of a 'selfish gene' propelling self-interested market activity.[84] In this way, Weber recognized and appreciated the 'heuristic significance of marginal utility' for decoding economic life, in the context of the specific '*cultural-historical fact*' from which it springs – in other words, capitalism. Its 'explanatory relevance ... is grounded in the capitalist epoch', and that alone.[85] Weber argued that it could not be considered outside of this context as a 'perennial phenomena', and needed to be analysed socially, historically and institutionally as it is produced and reproduced in the here and now, and with it the conditions it describes, reflects and helps bring into existence.[86] This exposes rational economic behaviour to be far from the 'individual trait rooted in psychology or biology' that hamfisted attempts to ascertain value and utility hold it to be.[87] Rather, it is 'a social-institutional property' far harder to capture and operationalize in schemes of quantitative research and inquiry. Having freed themselves of the compulsion to measure something that simply is not there, other 'social' theories may be much better placed to allow us to decode value in its everyday appearance.

* * * *

The concept of utility, partly successfully, establishes the possibility for a 'field' understanding of value, in that 'Utility is not a "stuff" or liquid and neither is the somewhat spectral neoclassical economic man'. Both, rather, 'are a field of possibilities that can characterize an empty commodity space' between the elements of which the relationship of value is forged.[88] This relationship is social, however – a fact that neoclassical economics cannot grasp. If the appropriation of metaphors sourced from physics was a means by which to 'discover the hidden fundamental natural determinants of value that lay behind the veil of everyday phenomena of money prices and incomes'– the essence of the value problematic to which all theories of it are addressed – then 'Utility as a field of scalar potential fit that pattern quite nicely'.[89] Moreover, at various points, the utility theory of value presents the opportunity to surpass attempts to ground value in some mystical substance intrinsic to the thing itself and scrutinize the true relationality of the ascription of monetary worth to goods and services by means of price. The 'dinner-table demonstration' of diminishing marginal utility as relating to individual everyday exchanges does not capture the scope of the theory insofar as it is really concerned with patterns, and not individual episodes, of consumption – the time rate of purchase and consumption, for instance, and not specifically whether an individual purchases one item over another.[90] Utility theory has the potential to widen our perspective on value beyond the thing itself and its individual consumer to the relation of each with the sum of things and individuals as a whole.

Moreover, neoclassical economics commendably freed itself of productivist illusions, thinking it 'a fallacy to indict any economic activity as simultaneously necessary-but-intermediate and yet unproductive', as, we might add, traditionalist Marxism is wont to do with fields such as the circulation of goods by means as diverse as marketing and transportation.[91] In this, there is a certain intellectual liberation in the fully fledged attack on productivism launched in utility theory. Only what legally retails on the market bears value. The burden of productivity falls not upon anything intrinsic to the production process itself, least of all upon workers held accountable for their lack of productiveness and subject to all the intensification Marx describes. Rather, whether something has value or is productive or not is determined solely in the setting of prices in the marketplace. The distinction between productive and unproductive is abolished in anything other than an abstract and retrospective sense insofar as 'since every sector that produces for the market exchanges its products ... there are few definitively unproductive sectors' – or even none at all.[92] It is far harder to force the divisive politics of productive and unproductive into the conceptual framework of such a laissez-faire way of understanding value. However, it should be noted that this potential has not prevented free-market economies underpinned by neoclassical notions of value from harbouring a politics of 'austerity populism', based on the celebration of 'wealth creators' and the suspicion of so-called 'benefit scroungers' and other purportedly 'unproductive' groups.[93] This highlights how, where Marxist theories of value had attributed to labour all powers of value creation, partly out of political expediency, marginalism has a tendency to do much the same but in the other direction, wary of granting to labour a right to the whole product and celebrating the capitalist instead.

Thus, whilst utility theory casts off the baggage of productivism to some extent, it is not without some sizeable issues of its own. In this and other respects, the potential of marginalism fared better on paper than it did in practice. In the steps it takes towards uncovering the social determinants of value, marginal utility theory falls victim to a circularity as debilitating as that found in other theories of value. The 'tastes and capacities' of actors incorporated in the constitution of value are conditioned by 'initial endowments of income and preference' that are themselves the result of previous valuations and demarcations of income into wages and profits arbitrated in the struggle of competing conceptualizations of value held by different actors. As a consequence, 'this endless regress deprives the array of simultaneous equations of the very thing needed to establish order – namely, a knowable, objective starting point or premise'. What is more, the antagonistic class basis through which value is a thing at stake at all in capitalist society is consciously elided, preventing any means of understanding or explaining the differential social conditions and circumstances that impact upon 'tastes and capacities' in the first place. Indeed, this is perhaps one of its selling points to its advocates, insofar as 'the utility approach to price ... recommends itself because it avoids troublesome considerations of class conflict and cooperation as the fundamental problem of social order, and puts in their place a view of social order as the outcome of individuals contending for pleasure or avoiding pain in an environment of scarcity'.[94]

Marginalism thus possesses an asocial and overly individualistic way of understanding the world. Taking price at face value as a measure of what things are worth stifles the capacity for contestation over value as a socio-political and normative category. This social and political dimension is absent in a theory that sees no value-creating role for government, for instance – a denial that itself has had tremendous real-world efficacy in political projects of the centre and right.[95] Such a view is incapable of capturing the active role of the state and other institutions in the determination and regulation of value and price, as well as the constitution and maintenance of the social conditions that make possible and reproduce a society based on the rule of value. The incapacity of marginalism to allow adequately for this antagonistic context owes to the idealistic and rationalistic assumptions core to its peculiarly scientistic approach to economic phenomena. For price determination to work in the way it proposes, humans are cast as 'one-dimensional utility calculators' capable of seamlessly rationalizing their best interests. Moreover, these actors must operate in conditions of perfect competition and equilibrium where supply and demand exist in a perfect harmony untroubled by interference from monopolies or states.[96]

The difference with Marxism, in this sense, rests less in how value is understood as a determined phenomenon, than in the constitution and determination of value as a historically specific social form assumed by a similarly historically specific set of antagonistic social relations that sit well beyond the purview of utility theory and its individualistic, atomized understanding of human life. In this sense, new readings of Marxian value theory, such as those covered in the previous chapter, combine an appreciation of the 'subjective' aspects of value with a more rigorous conception of the *objectivity* that grounds them and into which they disappear.[97] Such approaches, unlike marginalism, suggest that value is imbricated in other social forms expressing the same relations – the state, money, labour – which exceed the capacity of a narrowly economic frame of reference to capture them adequately. In this way, a fully social relational vision of value would take in society and its institutions as a whole, the implication of value within which is not exhausted in economic explanations alone.

4

Value and Institutions

Having considered the strengths and limitations of the leading currents of value inquiry, this chapter will chart the search for a value theory free of physical metaphor, whether field or substance, and for a 'social' theory that situates value in its imbrication within *institutions* instead.[1] We consider how a 'social' approach to value provides an alternative to prevailing approaches rooted in the humanities and social sciences.[2]

The oldest 'social' theory of value is the *normative* approach, which establishes a political or moral standard or basis for the ascription of worth to things or principles. Schumpeter wrote that 'Preoccupation with the ethics of pricing ... is precisely one of the strongest motives a man can have for analyzing actual market mechanisms'.[3] This approach can be associated with Aristotle, who stands at the inception of a subterranean tradition of value inquiry that holds up value to scrutiny as subject to political or social contestation.[4] In his conceptualization of value as centring on 'equivalence in exchange', Aristotle suggested that value was not intrinsic to commodities themselves but derived from a relational sphere – what in ancient Greece was called the *nomos*. This was 'rooted not in the material sphere of consumption and production, but in the broader social-legal-historical institutions of society'. This exposes value to scrutiny not as an 'objective substance' secreted in 'quanta that cannot be shown to exist, and of which no-one – not even those who need to know them in order to set prices

– has the slightest idea', but rather as 'the outcome of social struggles and cooperation' itself.[5]

In this sense, in Aristotle, we find not only the 'embryo of the Western value concept' noted earlier, but also that of its alternative. This owes to Aristotle's non-quantitative appreciation of value that permits 'no conserved entity' capable of 'reifying' value. Aristotle's monetary understanding of value opened up a social, and not economic, line of enquiry. Money, value's representative, is 'something intrinsically unstable because the function it performs' – that of commensurating heterogeneous things and quantities – 'is likewise unstable, unnatural'.[6] Owing to the instability of the conceptual material with which it works, the normative approach has the virtue of appreciating the role of *valuation*, 'a haunting but unacknowledged presence in all conceptions of value', and the role of *institutions* in its performance.[7] This is central to the 'social' theory of value charted here.

One form in which something resembling a 'social' theory of value has been taken up in recent years is in the academically voguish 'Sociology of Valuation and Evaluation' (SVE).[8] The second part of the chapter offers a critical overview of SVE, acknowledging its advances in promoting a notion of value grounded in social processes, but also highlighting the weakness of adopting an acritical understanding that limits its ability to appreciate value's full social and political significance. Sticking with the concept of 'performativity' found in the sociological literature, we close this chapter by considering what institutionalist and normative theories of value can tell us about the contemporary politics of value and productiveness, specifically in the context of national populism and its expressions at the level of the state. In so doing, we will encounter the urgency of value theory not only as a topic of academic inquiry, but as a 'performative' intervention into political and social life itself.

A Social Theory of Value

As we have seen so far, the rise of both substantialist and relational theories of value reflected changes in natural sciences, positing underpinning principles based in the idea of energy as either something conserved or something occupying a field of forces. A social theory of value, meanwhile, avoids all such scientific analogy, locating the principles that underpin value not in science or nature but in 'social institutions'. Both in the analysis of value theory as reflecting changes in natural science, and in the turn to institutions as a prism through which to view value, such a position is associated with the American institutionalism, whose most famous exponent was Thorstein Veblen. Hallmark contributions foundational to institutionalism, each seeking in their own way to understand value in the context of social institutions, include the study of accounting conventions conducted by Werner Sombart and the critique of the legal structure of property rights found in the work of John Commons.[9] Rather than value as something intrinsic to things or the relationships between them, a social theory of value is concerned instead with value as it relates to practices and processes of commensurating different things as somehow the same. This is not an economic matter alone: 'Value, as everyone knows, is about prices; but it is also about much more than prices. It analyses fundamental beliefs concerning why seemingly diverse objects and human endeavours are comparable; and even more outlandishly, how such comparisons can be reduced to a single common denominator of *number*.[10] The sameness that facilitates comparison and commensuration is not a property of things themselves, nor exclusively a mere operation of human reason allowing us to make our way through the world and meaningfully assemble the chaos of reality, but also a process whose underpinning assumptions about sameness and difference are 'assigned by human institutions' that are themselves simultaneously stabilized by the same classificatory assumptions.[11] From this perspective, theories of value that attempt to root themselves in natural metaphors are both a result of the institutional shaping of our expectations of sameness and difference, and a stabilizing component of those self-same institutions, telling a story to sell their timeless and asocial existence.

In considering how value stabilizes and is stabilized by society, this institutional perspective recognizes the fact that, independent of whether value is 'true' or 'false', it impacts upon our lives nonetheless. By seeking an explanation of value as part of the stabilization and reproduction of society itself – not always functionally, but in contradiction of the needs of that society – the social theory of value captures that value may not be something we can see or touch but it persists nonetheless, through the effect it wields on us at work in the wages we are paid, at home in the things we buy to eat and subsist, and in the wider economy as a whole in everything from the welfare system to the pension funds on which we depend to live long and fulfilled lives. Value *matters*, even if it has no *matter* at all.

But the social theory of value that we find in institutionalism goes further than connecting value solely with the imperatives of sheer survival. For Veblen, in his most famous work *The Theory of the Leisure Class*, 'nothing was purchased merely for its ostensible efficacy in the use intended; each and every purchase was a statement about the individual engaging in the transaction meant as a signification of that person's place in the culture's scheme of valuation'. From this, we can extract and take forward an 'undeveloped insight' of this work: 'that semiotic elements are inextricably entangled in the efficacy and use of any commodity'.[12] In short, 'In any valuation, the personal and the social are endlessly layered between acts of interpretation and signification'. This has implications for how other accounts of value are understood. For instance, as concerns neoclassical economics, it exposes how the 'maximization of any notional utility is persistently compromised by context'. And, for classical substantialist accounts, and the most orthodox variants of Marxist value inquiry, it suggests that value is not a quantity imparted to the product, but something registered between people and products in society at large.

In this way, the commensurability on which value rests is not something intrinsic to the commodity or its consumer, but, rather, subject to how the commodity is 'continually constructed and deconstructed and reconstructed in the process of market operation' between buyer, seller and the thing exchanged. In this lies the 'first assertion of a social theory of value': that the attributes of a commodity that bestow upon it a value are themselves socially constructed. This extends to the quantitative and mathematical formulae used to comprehend value, insofar as they are 'imposed upon

some arbitrary subset of the entire constellation of phenom-
enological peculiarities found there, in order to endow that
category with an "identity"', the ascription of which to a
reality initially resistant to quantification is the first step
towards the subsumption of that commodity 'under the
structures of value'. [13]

We might think of a number of practices that help bring
things under the sign of value in such a way: regional appel-
lations for wine, cheese or cured meats, for example, or,
less obviously, 'the apprenticeships of the medieval guild',
'the enforced standardization of machine manufacture' and
the 'modern cajolery of advertising', and, moreover, the
metric system, an instance of standardization central to the
'spread of the market'. These institutionalized standardiza-
tions, inside the workplace and outside in the market and
society as a whole, incorporate quantification – or the ability
to quantify something in a commensurate way at all – as a
necessary first step, which opens up the study of value in
numerous directions across the entire circuit of production
and circulation.[14] And, in order for these standards of
commodification to be circumscribed and effected in the
bringing of diverse and incommensurable things under the
sign of value, a vast institutional framework must be set in
place to ensure their smooth running, which is where issues
of power, antagonism and conflict enter the frame, inviting
consideration of politics, governance and the rise and fall of
social movements oriented to the contestation of what should
and should not be valued, and how.

One of the earliest attempts within the institutionalist
paradigm to investigate how the setting of such standards
depends upon a concrete set of institutional principles and
actions was the aforementioned early-twentieth-century work
of Commons, which explored 'the legal system as a major
locus of the definition and stabilization of the concept of value
in a market economy'.[15] Looking askance at the 'unnatural'
situation whereby certain things become traded as value-
bearing commodities, Commons contended that those things,
when bought and sold on the market, are not the physical
entities themselves but, rather, *rights* associated with them.
And, because the commodified form of what is exchanged
is at root a *right* to usage or ownership, rather than the

simplistic appearance of the physical thing itself, those rights are contentious and contended inside and outside the operations of the market. For the institutionalists, this is principally a semiotic issue, but we could associate it more widely with social contestation about what should and should not be valued in monetary terms, or, where such terms are undisputed, struggles over the correct price to pay. Owing to the uncertain and contested status of commodities, the standards of what is and is not brought under the sign of value 'require endless intervention and adjudication by a constituted legal structure' charged with superintending the invariance of the process by which rights are assigned and distributed.[16]

For the social theory of value, the invariance guaranteed by these legal systems concerns the expression of value in *money* and no other medium. Indeed, the acceptance of the monetary character of value is what associates the social theory of value with the relational reading of Marx's value theory. Price is the only means we have by which to ascertain something's value in capitalist society. And money, for it to act as an effective expression of value, must be in some sense invariant. Because the value of money is itself 'socially constituted ... its invariance is not guaranteed by any "natural" ground, and must be continually maintained' by legal and political social institutions such as those studied by Commons and other institutionalists.[17] Such institutions circumscribe the conditions of the expansion of the monetary unit, through a variety of means, of which the most notable is debt creation, which, by introducing temporary and shifting but 'irreversible trading schemes through time', allows the achievement of 'mutual gain' beyond a purely zero-sum set of exchanges between buyers and sellers of commodities. This invariance of the monetary unit, in spite of any changes in the value of that unit, provides the basis through which the players in this game can claim and trade property rights to new and existing assets on some rubric of measure and commensurability, and its expansion the basis for the accrual of profit therein. The relevance of national and international institutional frameworks to this – both public and private, state and corporate – is clear here.

The 'price system', therefore, is central not just to commodity exchange but to a whole range of practices and processes of reckoning in capitalist society. It commensurates the relative sense of worth of one act or object with that of another. And, in order for it to establish such a reckoning, 'some forms of change have to be ignored, or bracketed, or exiled', and the mess of reality must be abstracted from in order to establish a metric. This is what institutional standardization allows: the strategic disregarding of certain elements of a thing or kind of thing in order to bring those things into relation with one another under the form of value. And, in this sense, the price system has an 'epistemic' role in establishing an invariant code for the commensuration on which value rests. The price system endures threats from the changing value of money, which affords market players the opportunity of profit required for the reproduction of the economy itself. Value's invariant – money – is expanded through the creation of debt, but this invariance is infringed by inflation. This is not, as in neoclassical economics, a working of some magical and inevitable model of human and systemic behaviour, but '*socially constructed*' and 'non-mechanical'. Within this uncertain and changeable situation, individual choices within a system of private exchanges exacerbate countervailing trends of debt and inflation to undermine invariance further. All this means that social institutions must step into the breach to superintend the maintenance of the invariant so that debt, inflation, value and so on can all 'be written in terms of the [same] unit at different dates'.[18] But, rather than something given or underlying towards which prices must be forcibly adjusted in a process of arbitrage, the determinants of this invariant are themselves determined in exchange – in other words, the measured and the measure are constructed in the same moment. We are, at this point, some way from both substantialist and neoclassical approaches to value. The social theory of value takes society as a whole as its touch-stone, and not any reified element therein.

* * * *

As an example of the possible directions in which such an analysis can be taken, one of the most provocative and elaborate extrapolations of the institutionalist approach to value in recent years is that of Jonathan Nitzan and Shimshon Bichler – a theory that might best be described as the 'power theory of value'. For Nitzan and Bichler, value represents the accumulation not of any variable determined in the production of goods and services, but of *power*. Power is expressed through the ability to gain a differential advantage through the price mechanism, and is an index of *control* over the economy as a whole, and the degree to which the capitalist can suppress the successful growth of this economy and keep it within strictly delimited productive bounds. If productivity is given 'free rein', then problems of overcapacity can come to afflict the share of capital flowing to those who already own it.[19]

This perspective rests upon a conflict conceptually derived from Veblen, the father of institutionalism. This is the conflict between, on the one side, 'business' and 'power', and, on the other, 'industry' and 'creativity'.[20] Veblen placed the conflict between creativity and power at the centre of his analysis of human society. In the capitalist epoch, this conflict takes the appearance of the struggle between industry and business. 'Industry' is the collective and collaborative satisfaction of life's wants and necessities. This is achieved by means of ever greater synchronicity and coordination of production and consumption chains. 'Business', however, thrives on antagonistic relationships of conflict, tension and struggle. These antagonistic relationships are between capitalists themselves and between capitalists and society. Most of all, it thrives on the conflict between itself and industry.[21] In the context of this conflict, Veblen suggests that business earnings do not arise from greater efficiency or productivity. Rather, they arise from the sabotage of the creativity of industry and other businesses.[22]

In Nitzan and Bichler's extension of Veblen's work, accumulation of capital is simultaneously the accumulation of power. It thus represents the ability of capitalists and corporations to 'control, shape and transform society'. This is attempted in and against a context of conflict and opposition. This accumulation is therefore relative and, crucially, differential. It does not rely upon 'growth' in the economy as a whole, as is usually imagined. Rather, it depends upon the sabotage of growth in the name of competitive advantage.[23]

In expressing power, therefore, value does not relate to material production, real assets or number of employees. Rather, pecuniary earnings – the appearance that capital takes – are a 'symbolic representation' of success in a *struggle*. This struggle is among and between capitalists and corporations to 'shape and restructure' society. Most importantly, success in this struggle relies upon the ability to 'subjugate creativity to power'. This latter ambition actively militates against material, 'productive' activities and assets.[24] Value stands as a referent for itself and no other: sheer political, social and economic power that makes clear the link between the semiotic, the social and the material at which the institutionalist 'social' theory of value grasps.

* * * *

There are criticisms that can be made of the 'social theory of value' approach. The political content of social or 'normative' approaches suggests that, say, the value of the wage can be contested and reconfigured, whereas marginal utility theory would argue that the setting of a value is simply the sum of subjective choices made by rational actors in the market.[25] Meanwhile, substantialist approaches, which seek to locate the source of value in a fixed 'moral element or substance discoverable within the economic world', would see in the normative approach an untenable appeal to shifting principles subject to change and overhaul. But, all in all, institutionalism provides an open, operationalizable mode of value inquiry which overcomes many of the impasses of other approaches. However, as we will see next, some applications of its principles, where uprooted from a clear sense of social contestation and institutional force and power, expose blindspots in the way antagonistic social dynamics are captured in the study of 'valuation' as an institutional process.

Sociology of Valuation and Evaluation

Emerging from the meeting of French critical sociology, Deweyan pragmatism, post-structuralist theory and the so-called 'practice turn', the Sociology of Valuation and Evaluation contends that value does not rest within any commodity but, rather, is determined in the relationship between them, the people who produce and consume them, and the particular social practices from which they spring.[26] Such arguments have older antecedents, as we have seen – not least Aristotle, who, looking out upon a society in which money was playing an increasingly important socially synthetic role, posed the problem of value in terms of the equivalence exchange posits between diverse things, and not as anything intrinsic to them. The most fully realized vision of Marx's critique of political economy, the first volume of *Capital*, arrives at a somewhat similar 'social' and exchange-oriented perspective. The SVE, meanwhile, occupies a position less informed by materialist critical theory.

One of the foundational influences upon SVE is the work of Arjun Appadurai.[27] Influenced by Jean Baudrillard's critique of substantialism and productivism, which we examined in the first chapter, Appadurai provides useful correctives to some of the more wilful inaccuracies of orthodox Marxist thinking on value, and has grown in stature in contemporary economic sociology as a foundational scholar of the nascent 'valuation studies' approach. In setting forth this conception of value as something socially ascribed, Appadurai draws upon Georg Simmel's philosophy of money.[28] Like the 'subjective' theories of value explored earlier, Simmel considered value to be a subjective 'judgement' made about something, rather than 'an inherent property'. This subjectivity is provisional, contingent and inessential, but it is its nature as such that renders it worthy of study. In line with this, and what Appadurai attempts to do – and where his approach is most useful – is to explore how the relationship between commodities, exchange and value operates in practice as a lived social process. For Appadurai, the thing that functions to render an exchange productive of value is *politics*, enacted through the 'social lives' of commodities.[29] As Appadurai writes, politics, as the 'relations, assumptions, and contests pertaining to power', associates value with the 'mundane, day-to-day, small-scale exchanges of things' in everyday life, constructing frameworks that govern 'what is desirable', the proportion in which things exchange, and 'who is permitted to exercise

... effective demand in what circumstances'. The 'politics' here concern the 'relations of privilege and social control' on which such decisions rest, and over which conflicts arise, reshaping the existing frameworks of pricing, bargaining and so on.[30]

It is therefore the way in which 'economic objects circulate in different *regimes of value* in space and time' that constitutes the focus of this strand of value theory.[31] The economic objects – the *things* themselves – must be 'followed' through society in order to uncover the 'meanings' they assume at different points in time. In this way, Appadurai contends that it is necessary to break with productivist approaches to the creation of material things and their value, and instead focus on the '*total* trajectory' commodities follow 'from production, through exchange/distribution, to consumption'.[32] By tracing the 'trajectories' of economic objects through society, we can most clearly see the way in which human subjective judgements – 'transactions and calculations' – apply themselves to these objects at different junctures and, as Appadurai puts it, 'enliven things'. Appadurai suggests that this approach is informed by a dual perspective. From a theoretical point of view, the determination of value is taken to occur solely in the domain of human social activity. But from a *methodological* point of view, this determination can only be ascertained by a focus upon the specific 'things-in-motion' to which it is applied. Temporarily fixed in place as a lens on the relations that constitute them, the things-in-motion therefore 'illuminate their human and social context'.[33]

In order for this to happen, we must 'approach commodities as things in a certain situation, a situation that can characterize many different kinds of thing, at different points in their social lives'. For Appadurai, this specifically requires 'looking at the commodity potential' of a given thing. Thus, the method seeks snapshots of objects in their social context at the time of what Appadurai calls the 'commodity situation': that juncture in the social life of the thing 'in which its exchangeability (past, present, or future) for some other thing is its socially relevant feature'. This 'situation' can be broken down into three elements, consisting of a 'processual model of commoditization' inspired by Simmel's Aristotelian presentation of things moving 'in and out of the commodity state'.[34] The first is the 'commodity phase', into which a thing enters over the course of its social life. The second is the 'commodity candidacy' of that thing, which refers to 'the standards and criteria (symbolic, classificatory, and moral) that define the exchangeability of things in any particular social and historical context'. It is these exchange conventions to which parties comply that Appadurai refers to as 'regimes of value'.[35] The third element is the 'commodity context' into which the thing enters.[36]

* * * *

Stimulated in part by Appadurai's work on the social lives of commodities and 'regimes of value', the field of 'valuation studies' represents a growing body of research which offers considerable overlap with the aims and aspirations of some of the relational, 'field' theories of value covered elsewhere in this book, although not without important differences. Valuation studies has as its focus the practices and processes by which things are rendered valuable, as part of a wider 'pragmatic turn' in the study of economic activity.[37] Pragmatism, here, alludes to the work of John Dewey – specifically, his work on value.[38] What renders this orientation 'pragmatic' is its refusal to apply ex-ante explanations and a stance of anti-essentialism towards the uncertain social phenomena studied, in which the agency of actors renders meaningful the reality in which they move.[39] The pragmatic turn has been a productive outlet for empirical investigations of 'multiple regimes of worth or multiple conventions of valuation', including practices of testing, verification, calculation, metrics and documentation in a range of organizational settings.[40]

Specifically, focus has fallen upon 'the materiality of economic settings and devices'.[41] This is exemplified in the conception of the *market device*, which is taken to refer to 'the material and discursive assemblages that intervene in the construction of markets'. Examples include 'analytical techniques', 'pricing models', 'merchandising tools' and 'trading protocols'. The theoretical tool of the 'device', it is suggested, is a useful way of bringing 'objects' 'inside sociological analysis', treated not as inanimate but as possessing agency, whether this is instrumentally as a means of help, or deterministically through a relation of force.[42] For instance, the shopping cart is a device that 'reconfigures what shopping is (and what shoppers can do)', just as the stock ticker 'is a telecommunication device that reconfigures what trading is (and what traders are) in financial markets'. [43]

According to Muniesa et al., the concept of market devices can offer a good way of thinking through the issue of abstraction, also a key focus for the Marxian 'field' theory of value encountered earlier. Abstraction has been central to many analyses of what Muniesa and his collaborators label 'monetary mediations, mercantile enterprises and capitalistic forms'. Through the prism of the device, abstraction can be seen as an 'action' of extracting something from its context, as suggested by its etymology: *abs* (away), *trahere* (tract). In this sense, to abstract 'is to transport into a formal, calculative space'. The *agencements* of the market are formed of 'abstractive calculative devices' such as 'pricing techniques, accounting methods, monitoring instruments, trading protocols and benchmarking procedures'. Economists themselves are abstractive and calculative devices.[44] Such a picture of economic activity opens up a deeper interrogation of not only the social conditions that shape qualification and quantification, but their technical dimensions too – in other words, how they are 'tinkered with, adjusted and calibrated', and how this in turn affects how 'persons and things are translated into calculative and calculable beings'.[45]

In theorizing the calculative dimension of 'technical and material elements or devices' and the performative role they play in the practice of valuation, the empirical and theoretical work of Michel Callon and his associates has been pivotal – an approach broadly captured in the catch-all term 'cultural economy'.[46] In its conceptualization of qualification, valuation and 'economisation', this literature builds on Pierre Bourdieu's theorization of cultural intermediation.[47] Bourdieu's cultural intermediaries are members of a 'new petite bourgeoisie' working in 'occupations involving presentation and representation' and 'institutions providing symbolic goods and services'.[48] Cultural intermediation dynamically connects production and consumption, with cultural intermediaries themselves 'productive consumers': their own consumption is integral to their work in the sphere of production.[49] In this relationship, they intermediate between the two realms. The cultural economy approach develops Bourdieu's insights by grounding cultural intermediation in a framework of practices that work upon things to make them objects of commodification and consumption. This extends to a focus on the *actors* responsible for calculating, granting and communicating the value of things. For the cultural economy approach, 'cultural intermediaries produce and reproduce the hinges between culture and economy' by 'impact[ing] upon others' perceptions of value' in order to 'construct new meanings of good/practices and their value'. This extends to 'frontline service intermediaries' – i.e. those who deliver a cultural good or service, who help 'purchasing decisions materialize' in interaction with the end consumer.[50] This rests upon a process of 'economisation'. For instance, a 'tree growing wild ... may not be an economic thing but it may become one if parcelled as real estate or cut as timber', which necessitates the prior 'qualification' of its characteristics as a potential commodity, which narrates its 'detach[ment] from the seller's world' and entry into that of the buyer.[51]

Value is thus seen in the cultural economy approach as a matter of perceptions and 'meanings'.[52] Noting the insufficiency of a purely discursive or technical approach to value, a string of critiques of this set of approaches centre on their lack of engagement with any structural forms of power, their reluctance to consider the possibility of societal alternatives, their deterministic erasure of human contestation from social change in favour of non-human 'actors', and their elision of abstract processes of capitalist social mediation in the constitution of markets.[53] In these respects, the approach tends to leave unchecked the social relations that make value as a social form possible. In combining the acritical theory of value of Callon et al., which focuses on the practices and devices of valuation, with the conceptualization of social composition found in Bourdieu's theory of cultural intermediaries, the cultural economy approach deprives itself of a theoretical basis to articulate social antagonism and contestation in and around value. Bourdieu's class theory charts a path to nowhere in this respect. One of the central insights of

Bourdieu's theory is that the productive identities of cultural intermediaries draw upon and make use of their identities as consumers. Cultural intermediaries 'accomplish the objective orchestration between production and consumption'.[54] This occurs not only in work but in life. Their class position within what Bourdieu calls the 'new petite bourgeoisie' requires them to 'assuage subjective anxieties about class mobility'. This they do by shoring up their status through the consumption of social goods. At the same time as reproducing themselves as class actors, they reproduce the 'consumer economy' on which this tradition of value theory focuses. Thus, class is not a critical concept for Bourdieu, destructive and to be destroyed, but a Weberian matter of status and position, to which 'new petite bourgeois' social agents aspire.[55] As in Weber, Bourdieu's theory focuses on the way in which a given set of workers 'achieve a favourable market situation as traders of their own labour power'.[56] This situation is seen as uncompromised and unproblematic. For Weber, class collectivities form around shared lifestyles, ethics and a sense of 'status honour'.[57] This sees class position as in some way *positive*, and value as imbued with a kind of spirit stemming from this positivity.

Indeed, Bourdieu's redefinition of contemporary class structure around the ownership of different kinds of economic, social and cultural 'capital' is akin to the substantialist sleight of hand through which Smith associated different productive and unproductive class interests with their relationships to kinds of economic revenue.[58] Notably, the Great British Class Survey drew upon Bourdieu's differentiation of different kinds of capital – social, cultural, economic – to compile its breakdown of the contemporary British class system, spanning the precariat and the elite, with 'emergent service workers' and the 'established middle class' in between, among other such stratifications.[59] In characterizing the 'elite', the survey replaced exploitation with 'notions of "privilege" and "advantage"'.[60] In eliding the 'zero-sum game' of exploitation, this obliterates any conception of class as a relation between social actors that is both antagonistic *and* interdependent. The diverse forms of 'capital' that class actors possess are here *achieved* and not struggled over – different actors have different proportions of different kinds of capital, in a similar sense to that ascribed to Smith's value theory earlier. Moreover, they are achieved through consumption uprooted from the relationship with the buying and selling of labour power.

So, whereas Bourdieu sees working-class consumption of diversionary kitsch as a question of taste, education and refinement, a critical theorist such as Adorno sees it rooted in the alienation of the subject's labour and the 'lack of freedom and individuality'.[61] For Bourdieu, the conditions under which one consumes, as the criterion of class, are not determined by the class antagonism. But the constitutive nature of class in capitalist society means that 'capitalist production and capitalist consumption are differentially determined' and 'downright antagonistic'.[62] Production advances on the basis of an inequality that ensures the restricted capacity of one section of the population to consume. This antagonism is both the precondition of the sale of labour power, and immanent within the structure of the wage. Thus, according to Heinrich, the 'fundamental contradiction' of capitalism is 'between the tendency towards an unlimited production of surplus value, and the tendency towards a limited realization of it, based upon the "antagonistic conditions of distribution"'.[63] It is these 'antagonistic conditions' that are important to how we unpick the claims made about the relationship between consumption and production in theories of cultural economy and cultural intermediation. Value, for Marx's critique of political economy and the wider tradition of critical theory, contains and does not exclude this antagonistic context.

* * * *

Overall, then, the cultural economy approach, indicative of the wider SVE tradition as a whole, takes much for granted. It has no explanation of why it should be that people sell their potential to produce things for receipt of a wage used to buy other things produced by other people in the same situation. For this to happen, people must be initially and repeatedly deprived of independent means to produce and acquire that necessary to survive and enjoy life's possibilities and opportunities, whether individually or collectively. The foreshortened theory of value of this tradition gives no sense at all of the coercive and antagonistic social basis underlying the very possibility of there being a society based in value and commodities in the first place, nor the constraints that it places on the consumer economy that forms the focus of its empirical and theoretical attention.

Moreover, both Bourdieu and Callon, as well as the broader tradition they help inaugurate, tend to overlook 'human subjectivity', taking a 'technical and limited' perspective vis-à-vis how 'subjective processes and desires animate and inform social practice'. Ultimately, this blinds them to 'the articulation between subjectivity, the social trajectories and social formation of individuals and socio-technical devices'.[64] For Callon's theory of valuation, the problem is a lack of historicity, which prevents an understanding of how value relations develop in a 'social trajectory' of separation and domination. The elision of subjectivity and social trajectory gives no immediate or longer-view horizon to such speculations. In short, cultural economy elides the preconditions of the rule of value in class society's antagonistic undertow.

The Politics of Value

Turning back to institutionalism as a specific strand within the broader category of 'social' theories of value, and revisiting a minor theme of the book so far, we will close the chapter by considering one of the signal achievements of such a perspective. This is the attempt to situate theories of value not only in historical context according to scientific discoveries and so on, but within their political context, focusing on precisely *what* different theories of value do for and in the hands of different institutions, and how they respond to different institutional imperatives. Bringing together a way of framing value theory deployed throughout the book so far, we will see that this approach presents theories of value as themselves not only informed by socio-political and material circumstances, but also *performative*, in that they translate social and political imperatives into material reality. Theories influenced by the concrete conditions of the reproduction of social formations based on certain kinds of hegemonic class actors and the forms of capital with which they are associated feed into measures of value which do not merely passively reflect reality but performatively shape it. In turn, they then influence the further development of theory in directions commensurate with the reproduction of the conditions of productiveness of the given context these measures have helped construct – and so on and so forth. Dialectically, therefore, ideas are materially determined, and themselves materially constitutive of reality itself.

For a thinker within the broad institutionalist tradition such as Mariana Mazzucato, the development of value theory is bound up with the institutions of capitalist society and capitalist economics, and the interests and actors represented in and by them. Mazzucato suggests that ideas of who and what create value have reflected shifts in the significance of certain sectors of the economy and the interests of sections of society that have stood to benefit from their ascendancy: 'from agricultural to industrial, or from a mass-production-based economy to one based on digital technology'.[65] For instance, as we have seen, the late nineteenth century saw a switch from 'objective' substantialist theories of value in which value (or rather labour) determined prices, to 'subjective' relational theories of value in which price determined value. Mazzucato relates this to the consolidation of capitalist class interests in the face of the growing claims made on value by the increasingly organized industrial proletariat. The latter laid claim to the Ricardian or Marxist labour theory of value as justification for redress from what was perceived as the theft of their time and the value they created. Indeed, as we have seen, at least some of the residual Ricardianism in Marx's own value theory owed to his attempts to render his output accessible and operationalizable in line with what he saw as the political expediencies of the time. According to Mazzucato, those opposed to the aspirations of the rising working class were concerned with conceptualizations of value that focused on price and exchange – the domain where their power was established and secure – rather than labour, which was increasingly at stake. The critic Edmund Wilson states the case in blunt terms: 'The economist tends to imagine that value … is something mainly created by the group to which he belongs or whose apologist he aims to be'. In this, however, the rise of neoclassical economics was no different to any other theory of value that had been before. Wilson continues:

> The stupider type of old-fashioned manufacturer was practically under the impression that he was creating both the product and the labor by supplying the brains and the capital which gave the factory hand his opportunity to work. The Fabian Socialists represented the middle-class British consumer, and they believed that the human being as consumer rather than as farm laborer or factory hand determined the value of commodities by his demand for them. Henry George, who as a poor printer in California had been appalled to see that land of plenty transformed into a merciless monopoly where the rich were crowding the poor off the earth, had been led to conceive all value as primarily derived from the land. Karl Marx, who was not only on the side of the worker but wanted to see him inherit the earth, asserted that all value was created by labor.[66]

However, it is not quite as simple as calling out a series of sophisticated intellectual conspiracies, or saying that theories reveal their theorists to be incapable of reasoning outside of their own political or economic interests – or, for that matter, that the economic 'base' crudely determines the ideological 'superstructure' of society. This would be no better than those substantialist value theories that productivistically see all social life as decided in the labour process. Rather, what these ideas represent at any one time is the form within which social relations appear necessary for the reproduction of society under present conditions. This works both ways, insofar as the theories do not merely reflect real circumstances, but structure them. This Mazzucato refers to as 'performativity', following in the rich stream of poststructuralist sociological thinking also inhabited by the SVE approach – although with arguably more incisive effect. Measures of value and what is and is not productive and unproductive of it cascade from theory into practice and back again. For instance, as neoclassical economics reshaped the understanding of value away from production and towards supply and demand and individual utility expressed in the sphere of exchange – such that 'what is bought has value' – phenomena like financial transactions were recoded as productive activities where they were once classed as unproductive, with a commensurate impact on policymaking.[67]

Likewise, substantialist theories of value presupposed on wage labour, and subjective theories presupposed on price, each translate into measures such as GDP, which exclude the vast amount of unremunerated or poorly remunerated caring, cooking and cleaning work that plays a pivotal, but often gendered and racialized, role in ensuring the social reproduction of society itself. Such work falls under the flag neither of waged labour in the sphere of production nor of a service exchanged for money, its uneven burden left unrecognized. As Robert Kurz and Roswitha Scholz have shown, the fetishistic appearance abstract labour assumes in the form of value implies that production is dissociated from other spheres of activity such as reproduction. This simultaneously dissociates the gendered and racialized identities associated with each sphere. The sphere of production and the rights that accrue to the formally free seller of labour power are subsequently associated with a 'white Western male subject' engaged in waged labour productive of value.[68] Hence, value is not a neutral economic category, but one attributed and appropriated on the basis of ascribed social differences.

Whilst much work remains undervalued or unremunerated on the basis of these differences, the hegemony of marginal utility theory in capitalist society means that the achievement of a high wage, irrespective of the social consequences, confers upon labour productiveness and worth simply by virtue of the price it makes on the market. Whilst this at least has the merit of capturing accurately the unrelenting character of the rule of value in capitalist society, and preserves a kind of liberty free from state diktat in determining what is and is not a worthwhile expenditure of time and effort, it nonetheless carries with it a political and institutional constitution that the social or 'normative' strands of value theory described above are distinguished by reckoning with. The normative quality that value has in this regard marks it out as a space not of neutral objectivity, but of contestation and struggle, up for grabs. This normativity is not a post-hoc assessment of transactions and measures, but itself makes and remakes the lived reality of value and those subject to it. As Mazzucato writes, 'measurements are not neutral: they affect behaviour and vice versa'.[69]

Boundaries and continuums between productive and unproductive sectors and sections of society have a knock-on impact on decisions taken by governments and businesses – for instance, around the 'distribution of revenues between workers, public agencies, managers and shareholders'. The logic of performativity is that 'we behave as economic actors according to the vision of the world of those who devise accounting conventions' – in other words, the institutions that make the world go round. If these conventions imply a boundary between a productive many and an unproductive few, or a productive few and unproductive many, those who find themselves on the wrong side of the line may find themselves not just unaccounted for in GDP, but othered, uncatered for and even harried politically. Likewise, where GDP emphasizes the productiveness of some parts of the economy above others by virtue of activities being paid or extracting a price, but excludes others – such as care work, for instance – then policymakers, investors and other actors are incentivized to allocate support and resources accordingly.[70] As Mazzucato asserts, this can have the effect of sending out mistaken signals that lead the economy astray.

The institutionalization of a certain narrow array of normative ideas about productiveness and unproductiveness, Mazzucato suggests, has become much 'less explicit' and largely uncontested in the wake of the neoclassical ascendancy. In some ways, the latter potentiates a neutralizing effect on the divisive politics of productivism by moving its determination into the sphere of monetary exchange alone. Similarly, it has a depoliticizing effect on decisions over what should be produced and how, casting such questions out to the market. This, at least on paper, avoids criteria of productiveness being wielded by states to persecute outside groups for their lack of contribution to the productive community of the nation. Likewise – on paper at least – marginalism closes down debate about reward for contribution by displacing the determination of rewards to the market, where 'all income … is earned income' because it is only what sells that counts. Moreover – and again on paper – this way of framing value does not make a hospitable home for anti-rentier politics that poses rent-seekers against supposedly 'productive', profit-making enterprise. Theoretically, this escapes the substantialist suspicion of 'semi-parasitic behaviour' that 'extract[s] value from value-creating activity' without itself contributing. For marginalism, rentierism is merely a sub-optimal constraint on an impossible state of 'perfect competition'.[71]

But the permissive political environment made possible on paper by neoclassical economics does not pan out in practice, not least for those whose contribution is not valued to the same degree as those who stand to benefit most from the current state of things. Moreover, the hegemony of a market- and price-oriented view of value has not made any less persuasive the productivist politics of substantialist theories of value for those who seek to make political gain by building electoral and governmental programmes targeting a succession of 'unproductive' groups and individuals, rich and poor – whether benefit claimants, migrants, or imaginary 'globalist' elites.[72] These ideas persist in spite of – and sometimes in service of – the economic consensus. Meanwhile, Mazzucato argues, the false neutralization of the issue of productiveness, and its obscurity as a topic of formal economic debate, creates the space for rising industries and economic actors to engage in 'sustained lobbying' to persuade policymakers, regulatory bodies, governments and other parties to 'quietly place' them on the right side of the 'production boundary', with all the advantages this confers.[73]

It is fair to say that the politics of productiveness have returned with a vengeance in recent years. A recurring theme of the accounts offered by populists and their followers for industrial and economic decline is the unwanted presence of 'unproductive' groups, individuals and practices draining the moral and financial reserves of the nation and its people. The 'people' and their leaders are posed as productive and virtuous, making and building things and profiting from hard work that creates goods endowed with identifiable material value, rather than simply speculating or skimming value off the top. Classically, this posits a unity between industrialists and real-estate magnates and workers involved in certain industries or activities. Those who fall outside this rapidly eroding – if not already lost – industrial unity become the culprits of conspiratorial critiques of capitalism in the name of the nation and the people. Rubbing against the grain of the neoclassical embrace of free trade, this has brought back into play substantialist notions of value harking back to the 'balance of trade' mercantilism that saw value as a zero-sum game between nations, to be policed with tariffs and protectionist stimulus to domestic industry.[74] This politics builds walls to keep value within the nation, where, we are led to believe, it belongs.

Indeed, substantialism of one kind or another permeates the new populist politics of left and right alike. This is partly through a foreshortened class analysis that owes more to the 'general will' of Rousseau than it does to Marx.[75] Instead of seeing class as a negative relation to be abolished, it casts one partner in the relation as synonymous with the 'people' itself, to which the world is owed, having sprung from its creation. Where the triumph of the proletariat has historically been seen as inevitable, here the 'people' steps in to receive its rightful inheritance by vanquishing the 1%. Indeed, across the spectrum today, the Occupy idea of the '99%' translates into a formless but virtuous and productive people against an unproductive 1%. In its appeals against Wall Street bankers and political 'elites', this rhetoric unleashes a valorization of the 'national community of hard-working people' as a productive base over which the unproductive financial or political class rules.[76] The central idea is that wealth is something the 99% create, appropriated by the 1%. Mischaracterizing wealth and class in capitalist society, at its worst this seeps into anti-cosmopolitan conspiracy theorism, seeing money and value not as social categories immanent to capitalist society but as outside forces 'impos[ing] themselves with destructive force on a national people who appear thus as victims of cosmopolitan peddlers'.[77] Here, the class basis of Marx's labour theory of value is replaced by the figure of the 'people' appearing as the rhetorical agent of contemporary politics the world over. This leaves intact all of the labour theory of value's manifold theoretical and empirical issues whilst leaving behind, and politically disconnecting from, its moral *raison d'être*, replaced by an impossible but unimpeachable and productive 'people'.

The coincidence of this substantialist national populism, on the right at least, with wealthy strongmen such as Trump, reveals another aspect of contemporary productivism. As Frankfurt School critical theorists noted of the rise of Nazism in Weimar Germany, current events show that, rather than the 'exploitation of wage labor by capital, populist antisemitism and fascism portray wage labor and capital as productive allies in the struggle against parasitic politicians and bankers'.[78] Workers and industry combine against unproductive outsiders associated with global forces threatening the productive nation. As Adorno wrote, the 'diabolical image of harmony' the Nazis constructed was potentiated in the concentration and centralization of monopoly capital, the political response to which 'tends towards fascism' by 'mak[ing] people forget the actual existence of hostile classes' in a people united around the productive forces versus those of circulation and certain forms of capital. The command of large capitalists is such that, presenting itself as an institution rather than a social relation, the class antagonism is 'conjured out of existence' as proletarians and bourgeois alike rally around spellbound modes of critique and political action against it, in the name of the productive.[79]

Much productivist critique of capitalism in the contemporary climate is imbued with conspiracy theory. Present-day conspiracy theories that personify the ephemerality and intangibility of value in specific individuals and groups follow the template of classical conspiracy theories by seeking convenient alibis for novel, complex or inscrutable forces that exceed the capacity of actors to understand and critically comprehend them. They arise as attempts to explain phenomena that have a discernible effect, but without a clear culprit who can be held responsible – in short, social structures and relations such as value. Just like some of the value theories we have explored in this book, conspiracy theories respond to the threat of a class or social principle in its ascendancy or establishment. From conspiracy theory's modern inception, there is the focus on movements for social change, from the real-life Illuminati to the Freemasons to the Knights Templar, the latter of which exploited the trust in which they were held to make money from novel forms of banking where other forms of productive activity were impossible, raising the hackles of those fearing the wider changes encapsulating in new means of revenue-raising.[80] The Freemasons and the Illuminati, meanwhile – in their real-life existence, rather than the imaginary role ascribed them by conspiracy theory – represented the liberal political desires of the rising bourgeoisie. As these changes were under way, the targets of conspiracy theories were portrayed as undermining society from within. As today, conspiracy theories, personalized in the guise of individuals or groups, reified forms of wider changes in social relations as exchange and free labour overhauled feudal society, and bourgeois order replaced aristocratic dominion. But, with the establishment of bourgeois society, conspiracies tended to place a greater emphasis on external forces in a false attempt to confront the class antagonism. We see this today in the populist ideal of the hardworking and productive national people assailed by parasitical outsiders, as well as in the forms of left and right antisemitism discussed briefly at the end of chapter 2.

Aside from their obvious and deeply unfortunate real-world consequences, the trouble with such insider–outsider models for understanding productiveness and unproductiveness is their lack of a firm grasp on the social character of value as a category that does not consist within things, places, people or groups, but *between them*. Value represents a totality of relations that does not reduce to who 'takes' and who 'makes', insofar as many parties and institutions contribute to valorization – whether unpaid work to reproduce human life in the form of labour power, merchants who move goods to consumers, transportation companies who move consumers to goods, advertising agencies who emotionally move consumers to consume, or financiers whose investment instigates production processes to begin with.[81]

Something more is needed. If, as Marx's developed value theory holds, 'sensuous social practice subsists in and through the movement of supersensible economic things', individuals cannot be held responsible for the specific forms of value or wealth of which they are the objective representative, and through which they subsist 'on pain of ruin'. Moreover, 'the supersensible world is the world of sensuous human practice in inverted form'.[82] As such, the ascription of an all-encompassing global power to finance, ruling over human subjects, takes at face value the social forms assumed by social relations. The productivist conspiracy theorism that courses through contemporary populism therefore operates on a fetishization of social forms, and reification of social relations, masquerading as a critique of capitalist society. But, ultimately, it carries over wholesale its key category, value, which is deployed acritically and positively as something the 'good' popular subject produces, and on which the 'bad' elite leeches. One cannot 'oppose the fateful movement of coins' by criticizing the personifications of economic categories and their 'profit-making consciousness'.[83] Marx himself criticized those who 'make the individual responsible for relations whose creation he socially remains'.[84] Rather, we must critique 'the capitalistically organized social relations of human reproduction that assume the form of a movement of economic things, which objectify themselves in the person', rather than the person itself.[85] The name for this struggle, as we shall see in the next chapter, is value.

5

Value as Struggle

Throughout this book, we have used the incisive work of Philip Mirowski to articulate the historical shift from 'substance' theories of value to 'field' theories of value, and particularly the active and continuing tension between the two within the Marxian tradition of value theory.[1] Some in this tradition, however, have refuted the notion that there is a clean and easy split between substance and field, not only in Marx's work but more broadly in physics itself. Notably, George Caffentzis has pointed out that, reflecting the coexistence of, say, wave and particle in quantum mechanisms, substance and field concepts similarly coexist within Marx's value theory – for instance, in socially necessary labour time as something embedded in the labour process but determined outside it, or the use of the 'crystal' as an analogy for the way that abstract labour is represented in the commodity – not in direct contradiction but in a dialectical interrelationship that exposes Marx's theory as in some way consistent, rather than inconsistent as Mirowski claims.[2] In this respect, the dialectical method of Marx's *Capital* does not counterpose the appearance of value and the reality of labour, or value as a social form and the actual conditions of life it mediates. Rather, it suggests that the one is contained within the other.

This critique, as we shall see in this chapter, is expressed by Caffentzis and others in what we term, somewhat crudely, 'class struggle' theories of value that straddle the line between aspects of what was defined as the 'substantialist' Marx, focused on the labour process in determining value, and the 'relational' Marx, focused on the valorization process as a whole. As we will see, class struggle theories of value refute the simple distinction between physiological and social theories of value, and objective and subjective theories of value, by reinstating to the relational version of Marx's value theory presented in chapter 2 the centrality of class struggle to the constitution of capitalist society, the relevance of how exploitation is experienced and resisted in the labour process, and the practical existence assumed by abstract labour within production itself, rather than presenting it as something generated only in exchange.

The approaches covered in this chapter moor the understanding of value in a normative and social frame of analysis that addresses some of the impasses of the perspectives discussed in chapter 1 – specifically around class and the practical and political implications of conflict over value.[3] The approaches understand value as *struggle*, or, more precisely, a form assumed by – or a 'mode of existence' of – class struggle in capitalist society.[4] This insight unites the closely related theoretical schools of 'open' Marxism – whose principle theorists include Werner Bonefeld, Ana Dinerstein and John Holloway – and autonomist Marxism – whose principal theorists include the aforementioned Caffentzis, as well as Harry Cleaver and Massimo De Angelis.[5] We will also draw upon the sometimes countervailing theoretical strands of *Wertkritik* (or 'value critique') – the most notable representative of which is Robert Kurz – and the 'practical criticism' perspective associated here with Guido Starosta.[6] Part of a family of approaches also including the 'new reading' of Marx touched upon in chapter 2, these excitingly unorthodox reconstructions of Marx's value theory share a common origin in dissident libertarian or emancipatory strands of twentieth-century Marxism and critical theory in Europe – particularly Germany, France and Italy – the United States and Latin America.[7] This strand of Marxist theorizing is libertarian and emancipatory because it tends to reject the political implication of what we will label 'traditional Marxist' accounts, which bear the hallmark of a positive 'affirmation of the proletariat as producer of value' and the seizure of state power to facilitate its rightful ownership of the wealth produced. On this front, Marxism's chequered past in the hands of authoritarian state socialism is partly the result of a misinterpretation of Marx's theory of value as subject to such an affirmation of the production of value, rather than its 'radical negation', which is a key underpinning principle of the critical approaches to the theorization of value and labour in capitalist society discussed in this chapter, and more broadly in this book.[8]

Shorn of 'dogmatic certainties and naturalistic conceptions of society', for scholars rooted in the approaches synthesized in this chapter, Marx's critique of political economy is read as a critical theory of society, rather than 'one "economic theory" beside many others' – an alternative 'bundle of sociological and economic hypotheses'.[9] As we will see, the ultimately 'qualitative' and 'sociological' consequences of Marx's critique of political economy resound in the account of the 'social constitution' of value in the class antagonism, making clear its complexion as something much more than an economic theory.[10] This casts Marx's critique of political economy as 'a theory of historically specific social mediation' and the misapprehended expression of its 'surface forms' in economic thought.[11] This means that, contrary to approaches that prioritize historical materialism as a kind of economic determinism, Marx's critique of political economy is not an argument for the 'primacy of the economic', but, rather, concerns the 'social production and reproduction of the life of society as a whole'.[12]

In this perspective, the critique of political economy captures what classical political economy cannot: that 'human needs, labour and wealth always have specific social form and purpose'. For Marx, the historically specific forms of capitalist society 'are pervasive and of great consequence', reaching 'all the way down' into how the things we need to live are produced and how we attain them.[13] But they also reach all the way up, too, taking in an expansive terrain of mediations in their role 'as modes of existence' of the class relation under capitalism – not only 'the commodity-form, the value-form, the money-form, the wage-form' and so on, but the *state-form* as well, without losing focus on 'the struggle in which that relation consists'.[14] In turn, they open Marxian value theory beyond labour and exchange as economic moments and into their social relationship with life as a whole, through engagement with the means and processes through which we reproduce ourselves and others, and, in so doing, society itself. In this respect, this struggle-based theory of value connects with increasingly pressing issues of contemporary concern, not least the position of socially reproductive work based on a gender division of labour in underpinning the rule of value.

Social Constitution

History, wrote Adorno, 'is the history of class struggles'.[15] The class antagonism is constitutive of capitalist society, and what went before capitalism is not history, but prehistory.[16] Value can be said to be a *mode of existence* of class struggle, insofar as it represents a form of mediation within which the antagonistic social relations constitutive of capitalist society are both expressed and concealed. A 'mediation', in this sense, constitutes the relation between things via another 'intermediate' thing, in the same way as 'a rope linking two climbers is constitutive of the relation in which they stand'.[17] As a 'category of social mediation', value represents a 'non-empirical reality'.[18] But in such mediations, Marx writes, 'material relations between persons and social relations between things' appear precisely 'as what they are'.[19] It is precisely the non-empirical forms that mediate social life in capitalist society 'that first make possible an understanding of that which appears empirically', rooted as they are in human practice and lived experience.[20] The objective appearances assumed by capitalist social relations contain within them the essence of their antagonistic constitution in human practice. And this opens up the possibility of capturing these antagonisms as 'matters of experience'.[21] It is thus possible to move through form to grasp content. In 'Understanding the specific forms of society, we can understand the typical action of individuals; but starting with the action of individuals we will not understand the forms. Or we take them for granted, we don't see that such forms have to be explained', the social element at the core of economic categories being left unpicked.[22] Exploring how this illuminates our understanding of value as a 'mode of existence' assumed by struggle, in this chapter we connect the form analysis of the relational Marx presented earlier with the study of this empirical 'social core' at the heart of non-empirical economic categories. Rather than a logical derivation independent of social action, then, 'The analysis of the logical structure of the value-form is not to be separated from the analysis of its historical, social content'.[23]

Along these lines, Marx begins *Capital* with the commodity and goes on to 'elucidate a development that cannot simply be called economic, but rather is really the development of the commodity form as it moves', a development that takes in society as a whole.[24] Marx begins from the commodity, and not the social constitution of a society based on the buying and selling of labour power in and through the class antagonism. From this perspective, the historical specificity of capitalism consists in the way that wealth, broadly defined, takes on the social form of value, expressed in money and represented in what Marx opens *Capital* by calling the 'immense accumulation of commodities'.[25] But, for Marx, insofar as the man is the key to the understanding of the ape, he begins from the most developed social form of a set of social relations he progressively unveils as the work – in this case, *Capital* – goes on.[26] *Capital*'s chapter on primitive accumulation, in which Marx unfolds the historical constitution of the abstract categories covered in early chapters, does not arrive until the very end of the book. History 'does not precede the theoretical development, but rather follow[s] from it', and Marx uses this presentation to show that 'the separation of immediate producers from the means of production is the central historical precondition of the capitalist mode of production', and therefore of value.[27] For trade, exchange and money to be 'transformed into capital, the prerequisites for capitalist production must exist', and labour must be made to assume the social form of value, which, according to Marx, occurs 'as soon as men start to work for each other in any way'. For this to occur, as we saw in chapter 1, 'the owners of the means of production and subsistence [must] meet the free labourer selling his labour power'.[28] Dispossessed of the land and of any means of subsistence, formally free individuals are forced to sell their labour power to capitalists availed of the means of production. Sold on the labour market, their labour power becomes itself a commodity and the basis for other such commodities. In the context of such a society, riven by the class relation, exchange becomes 'the synthetic principle that immanently determines the connection of every social fact'.[29]

Whereas some interpretations of Marx conceptualize this process of primitive accumulation as a pre-capitalistic phenomenon belonging to the 'prehistory' of capitalist society, and others view it as a form of accumulation aimed at resolving capitalist crisis, the struggle theory of value reads dispossession as a persistent part of capitalism foundational to a society governed by value.[30] Private property and wage labour are continually generalized through the enforced dispossession of a majority of the world's inhabitants of the independent individual and collective means necessary to reproduce their conditions of living outside of the wage relationship. This relationship is mediated in the social form of value, through which 'Domination in capitalism ... is rooted in quasi-objective structures of compulsion constituted by determinate modes of practice, expressed by the categories of commodity and capital'.[31]

Importantly, such an understanding of social reproduction as continuingly central to the constitution of capitalism opens up the study of value to the insights of Marxist-feminism and what has become known as 'Social Reproduction Theory'.[32] These extend the understanding of the relationship between value, work and labour outward in such a way that 'the particular relation of capitalist work is not limited to wage-labourers in the commodity-producing sector of society, but includes also the non-waged proletariat' whose work, whilst unremunerated, still plays a part in reproducing the social basis and rule of value as a form assumed by human activity under capitalism.[33] This is indicative of how these readings of value as a historically specific social form embed within their conceptualization of value the constitution of capitalist society in a gendered set of relations around how human life as labour power is produced and reproduced, such that it can be sold on the market and engaged in the production of commodities itself – in other words, the 'conditions of possibility of labour-power' that lie in the unpaid labour of caring, cooking, cleaning and raising children, performed on the basis of a gendered and often racialized global division of labour.[34] As such, whilst the approaches covered here may reinstate to the study of value close attention to the classed social relations of production as opposed to an overly circulationist focus, this does not preclude, and indeed encourages, the extension of value theory to take account of the dimensions of gender and social reproduction in which value is socially constituted.

* * * *

In emphasizing the constitutive character of social differences and social conflicts in capitalist society, class struggle theories of value also intersect with the insights of Black Marxism in grasping the foundational role that unfree labour and dispossession play in continuing processes of primitive accumulation underpinned by racial domination.[35] As discussed in chapter 2, Marx saw slavery as not only pivotal in the transition from pre-capitalist modes of production to a society ruled and mediated by the value form, but a persistent presence subsumed and rearticulated within the development of capitalist social relations and social forms. But for Black Marxists, Marx's method of abstraction elides the concrete reality of racial domination in the constitution of the forms and categories with which *Capital* is preoccupied.[36] The traditional Marxist identification of homogeneous labour as 'the secret of the expression of value' has often been twinned with the idea that capitalist labour is characterized by 'formal freedom and equality' before the law, to the exclusion of states of unfree labour occupied by racialized surplus populations.[37] However, for Black Marxism, capitalism is always in some respect 'racial capitalism' insofar as, through ongoing primitive accumulation, it accumulates through dispossession based on social difference denominated in 'the unequal differentiation of human value'. Playing out in the accrual of 'uneven life chances' according to race, this is not restricted solely to 'white supremacist capitalist development' expressed in 'slavery, colonialism, genocide, incarceration regimes, migrant exploitation, and contemporary racial warfare', but appears also in less directly violent practices that 'value and devalue forms of humanity differentially' in line with capitalist logics.[38]

Unlike traditional Marxism, struggle-oriented theories of the value form, by associating capitalist society with generalized and indirect abstract forms of domination that subordinate specific and direct relationships between capital and workers, keep open theoretical space to accommodate the compatibility of capitalism with the persistence and reproduction of 'direct, overt forms of racial and gender domination' and the market-mediated management of populations subject to this domination.[39] In this way, there is nothing intrinsic to 'free labour' in the constitution of capitalism, insofar as the 'self-expansion of value' that characterizes capitalism is 'intrinsically indifferent to the [concrete] forms in which it dominates labour', whether free or unfree.[40] From this perspective, Marx's progressive uncovering of the social and political conditions that 'disappear' into the value form in *Capital* suggests that it is not as simple as separating out capitalism from the extra-economic coercion some associate only with prior modes of production. Where Marx describes how the 'Roman slave was held by chains' and the 'wage labourer is bound to his owner by invisible threads', it is not a simple transition from personalized forms of domination to impersonal as if one epoch could be neatly sliced from another, but also a dialectical subsumption of the former in the latter. As Sorentino writes, 'both slavery and wage labour preceded capitalism, only to be rearticulated by it', just as the impersonal abstract social domination characteristic of capitalism comfortably 'absorbed the slave' and continues to accommodate racialized and gender violence.[41] The value form conceals this dimension not simply as part of its pre-history, but as a continuing constitutive factor in its existence. By recognizing the violence and conflict concealed in the value form, class struggle theories of value can open up beyond class to incorporate other moments of social domination in capitalist society – not only around gender, but around race as well.

Value at Work

In viewing value as 'a mode of existence of the class struggle', approaches based on a 'class struggle theory of value' unite a form analysis of value with an analysis of the content of struggles at the point of production.[42] For the 'monetary' theory of value that represents the fullest development of Marx's work, the central 'expository motive' of Marx's value theory is the crucial question *'why this content assumes that form'* – in other words, 'the specific social character of commodity-producing labour'.[43] But the approaches presented in this chapter make a complementary but counter-vailing move of focusing on the content hypostatized in the form of value. In this, it follows Marx in ascribing agency not to 'some non-human source' in determining value, but to the activity of and relations between people.[44] The *form* of the relation might appear as a relation between non-human things (the commodities themselves), but its *content* is that of innumerable human actions. For Marx, the equivalence of commodities is 'only a representation in objects, an objective expression, of a relation between men, a social relation, the relationship of men to their reciprocal productive activity'.[45] But this does not mean that those relationships are entirely subsumed and diminish in tangibility or importance. As Marx writes of the commodity fetish, the money form, whilst abstract, contains within it the concrete roots of its creation, and 'it is precisely this finished form of the world of commodities – the money form – which conceals the social character of private labour and the social relations between the individual workers, by making those relations appear as relations between material objects, instead of revealing them plainly'.[46] As we shall see, labour in the production process already has this abstract social dimension, pending the full appearance of abstract labour in exchange, and it is in this respect that it is a locus for conflict and contestation.

The theory of value as a mode of existence of class struggle thus understands abstract labour as a concrete, practical category with an existence within production, rather than one that pertains only to circulation – in other words, the 'analytical representation of the antagonistic class relation of work'.[47] In this way, it treats abstract labour neither transhistorically – as might a Ricardian reading of value theory – nor as a logical derivation – as might the 'new reading' of Marx – but rather as a historically and socially specific phenomenon associated with work in capitalist society alone. Abstract labour is thus not a mental or intellectual category, but one that assumes a practical existence in the very content of the production process itself, with all the material hardship, indifference to human needs and human and natural suffering and degradation that this implies.[48] Specifically, abstract labour is here a social form forged not merely from the realm of exchange between capital and labour in the marketplace, but rather as the manifestation of the class antagonism between capitalist and worker in the sphere of production, a *'relation of struggle'*.[49]

Where circulationist approaches see the abstraction of labour stemming from its position in the market system of capitalism, for the 'class struggle' theory of value, labour is abstracted by its very existence as wage labour, as 'work exploited by capital'.[50] This is because 'the unity of production and circulation' is always 'centred on labour as both means and ends of exchange value', in that 'labour is the means by which to produce (exchange) value' in production, and constitutes 'the end (the "product") of (exchange) value' in circulation. In this way, the circuit of capital continues with each circulation presupposing the next round of production, with labour always as its aim and end.[51] In this sense, labour is in some way abstract right from the inception of production, owing to its status as wage labour, because capital is posited in its form as money right from the very beginning of the process. Through its positing as money at the beginning of a round of production, abstract labour is thus not a residue of the production process expressed in exchange, but rather a totality within which everything proceeds from start to finish. Production, in this sense, is not something that could be the same under a different set of social forms and relations, but represents the 'disembedded abstract space of business' specific to capitalism, wherein the value abstraction is established not after the fact in the market but in the sphere of production itself.[52]

In reinstating the sphere of production as a terrain for the abstraction of labour, class struggle theories of value thus hold that abstract labour is present at some point (or all points) of the production process and then finds itself carried over into the commodity.[53] Rather than coming to be abstract in exchange, then, this disputes a one-sidedly 'field' approach to Marx's value theory, suggesting that 'labour is abstract' from the off and '*therefore* it must take the form of value and be expressed in a sum of money'.[54] From this perspective, the dual character of labour refers not to 'two different activities' corresponding to its abstract and concrete poles, but 'an opposition within the same activity', i.e. 'capitalist work'.[55] Abstract labour is therefore not merely a 'validation relation' forged in circulation, but a relation of production and a '*substantial relation of subjugation*', and as such centres on the production process as itself a 'real abstraction' bearing not only a material and physical content, but social content too. Hence, it at once produces a spectral and 'ghostlike' objectivity – value – whilst also implying intense and deleterious consequences for resources both human and natural. From this perspective, banishing this spectral, ghostlike character solely to the circulation process, as do the relational theories of value examined in chapter 2, naturalizes production as itself a real abstraction, mistaking it for concrete labour pure and simple.[56] The reduction, witnessed in capitalist production, of human labour to a 'mere expenditure of physiological energy' is itself a social abstraction specific to the capitalist organization of labour-time as an emptied-out duration shorn of content and context.[57] What differentiates this from a purely 'physiological' approach to abstract labour as the substance of value is that the practical abstraction of labour undermines the 'sensuousness' of labour itself through the addition of elements that are not purely physical, such as '*subjective feelings* (boredom, indifference, suffering, etc.)' and a decision-making process over 'what, how much and how to produce' from which the worker is completely ostracized. The imposition of abstract labour within the labour process itself brings about the alienation of the worker from their labour, the real abstraction of concrete labour abstracting in turn from 'lived experience', burdening work itself with an 'emptiness of meaning' and a profound disharmony with 'human needs'.[58]

* * * *

On this account, following Caffentzis's critique of Mirowski with which the chapter began, value is in some respect both substantial and relational. Abstract labour, as a socially mediated 'substance', is present in production but conditioned by the wider set of exchange relations into which labour enters in capitalist society – in other words, the valorization process as a whole. The labour process, as we saw in chapter 2, is part of, and structured in line with the imperatives of, the valorization process. In this sense, for class struggle theories of value, value determines and 'organizes' labour, rather than the reverse, as is typically considered the case in the Marxist tradition.[59] Whilst 'value – market value – must be understood as emerging from relationships amongst people', value, 'having emerged from human relationships ... then turns around to dominate these relationships'. This manifests on the ground in the decisions managers make, who employ measures not in the pursuit of calculation or better understanding, but to 'drive change' and 'improve performance' – that is, 'to organize and to "determine" labour'. In particular, measurement plays an active and not passive role with reference to the labour it measures, and premonitorily commensurates 'value-producing labours' ahead of their final validation in the market:

> the measures thus constructed (and imposed) are not passive. Within the organization, they are wielded as management tools to (re)organize – or *determine* – labour, i.e. 'to improve productivity and efficiency'. Outside the organization, they are reflected in price levels, which, mediated by the competitive process and the market, influence or determine – the organization of labour elsewhere in the economy. (The external market validates – or not – the organization and determination of concrete labours within the organization.) As the McKinsey slogan puts it: *'everything can be measured and what gets measured gets managed'*.[60]

We saw in chapter 2 how new readings of Marx have stressed the centrality of the market in determining SNLT as a post-hoc measure to which labour is made subject in arbitrating its value-productiveness as abstract labour. Class struggle theories of value give a slightly different reading, in that the abstraction of labour is conceptualized as a process experienced in production. Despite its irreducibility to measure by 'clock or calendar', this proceeds by means of the measurement of time. As Cleaver asserts, 'the measure of abstract labour, its time, must be understood to be as much a social concept and phenomenon as is abstract labour itself', occupying the social mediation between concrete labour and value that is established through the progressive averaging of labours through the setting and meeting of SNLT.[61] Whereas, as we saw in chapter 2, some new readings of Marx suggest that this is not something lived but something retrospective, for the class struggle theory of value, SNLT is something subject to lived experience within the sphere of production itself. As Cleaver writes:

> the concern with abstract labour (value) drives capitalists to shape the division, and hence the very structure, of useful labour in order to realize the homogeneity of abstract labour. Because of this, *useful labour in capital must be seen as the very material out of which abstract labour is crafted.* The work that is imposed on people through the commodity-form, which constitutes the substance of value in capital, exists only in the fluid structure of concrete useful labour.[62]

Thus, abstract labour takes on an existence in the labour process through the measurement of SNLT as 'expended abstract-physical energy in time units' of concrete labour stripped of content. The abstract time of the valorization process, as the 'disembedded' functional sphere of business that unites production and circulation alike, is thus qualitatively different to the event- and task-based time of pre-capitalist society.[63] Value, therefore, structures the experience of everyday life and labour under capitalism, right down to the way that time passes.

Class Subjectivity

The imposition of SNLT upon the labour process centres on a struggle between how workers live and experience labour and its real abstraction in measure.[64] For some scholars of value as a mode of existence of struggle, this is experienced by workers as the transformation of 'doing' or 'power-to' into the 'done' or 'power-over'. For Holloway, human 'doing' – autonomous collective and individual activity geared towards some useful or pleasurable end – appears in capitalist society only in the mode of being 'denied' as wage labour. Owing to the constitution of capitalism in a set of antagonistic social relations, the human capacity to transform the world through work can only be expressed as wage labour. 'Power-to' (that is, the power to create) is transformed into the 'power-over' represented in abstract economic imperatives of value and profit. 'Human doing', in this sense, struggles against its subversion in the form of the accomplished organizational fact of the 'done' – abstract labour, the homogeneous, undifferentiated time of capitalist production.[65]

However, the case is never quite closed and domination never done and dusted, insofar as 'doing' or 'power-to' always represent a pole of struggle against their denial in the form they appear in as value in production – or, rather, abstract labour. This struggle occupies the terrain of time and its measurement insofar as the abstraction of labour proceeds in a 'time of reification' undermined by the 'time of insubordination' within which workers resist this abstraction. The former is the general 'uniform and continuous time' of capitalist valorization. As we have seen, labour must be, as far as possible, emptied of its specific content and divorced from its specific context in order to become measurable as abstract labour – in other words, that measured as SNLT. Within this abstract time, however, there persists a latent time of 'struggle over the reduction of human creativity into profit'. On the one hand, this human creativity 'can be realised only within the framework of a form of power that is alien to it'. This is because human activity in capitalist society is worthwhile and recognizable only via the process through which it is expressed in a product bearing a monetary value on the market. On the other hand, human creativity resists its 'negation' in capitalist production, its creativity chafing against the measures to which it is subject in the name of the valorization process. The vexed interrelationship between the 'time of reification' and the 'time of insubordination' renders capitalist social domination unstable and precarious. In this way, 'human creativity is a scandal because its potential for dysfunctionality inserts uncertainty into the "well-oiled" machinery of accumulation'. At the same time, capital relies upon it. This reliance upon human creativity, however, 'negat[es] its purpose', because the 'abstract temporality' to which labour must by necessity be rendered subject 'tends to annihilate' the creativity on which production rests. Thus, the capitalist negation of human doing as measurable abstract labour conducted in the 'time of reification' is marked by continuing conflict and contradiction – and, as we shall see in the next chapter, crisis.[66]

At the same time, the imposition of this time of abstract labour within the labour process exposes the contradictory character of class struggle in a society where we reproduce ourselves as labour power. Whilst the 'concrete expenditure of labour time' can only be fully validated as socially necessary after the fact in exchange, workers still suffer the high stakes of the common struggle to make it so in production. The conflicted interdependence produced by the social constitution of capitalist society in the class relation means that, 'on pain of ruin', all parties to production engage in the expenditure and management of labour 'in the hope that it will turn out to be socially necessary and that it will thus achieve value-validity in exchange with money'.[67] Both the capitalist and the worker rely on this validity in order for their conditions of living, buying and selling to be repro- duced. Often in contradiction with their mental and physical health, the worker has a vested interest in the validation of their labour as socially necessary.[68] In this way, social validity applies not only in the market, as we saw in chapter 2, but in the very 'form of the relations of production within which production takes place'.[69]

* * * *

Notwithstanding some important differences largely left untouched in this chapter, what we have grouped together here under the banner of the 'value as struggle' approach provides an important counterweight to overly circulationist accounts of Marx's value theory, such as those encountered in chapter 2, whilst still overcoming the impasses of a substantialist account in its recognition of the importance of the valorization process as the context within which labour takes place.[70] Moreover, in the respect to which they recognize the contradictory character of political subjectivity and class struggle in a world governed by abstract mediations, the approaches detailed above have been lauded for their escape from the 'naïve immediatism and subjectivism' of many contemporary radical left readings of Marx, as well as the 'fatalism and quietism' implied in more traditional Marxist perspectives.[71] However, they have been criticized for the lack of specificity with which they approach class struggle, and the lack of concreteness and realism in their hopeful appraisal of the capacity for emancipated human practice to spring forth in moments of demediation where the value abstraction is burst asunder.

In particular, by posing class struggle, and thus working-class subjectivity, as in some way prior to its mediation in the workplace, class struggle theories of value have been criticized for overlooking the way in which the specific form that value-producing labour takes in capitalist society ('the alienated value form of the product of labour') is ultimately blind to the 'material determination' which gives rise to the working class's subjectivity as such in the class struggle. Class struggle theories of value endow participants with a false attribute of freedom where really even the class struggle itself is determined by the *indirect* social relation that constitutes capitalism, and abstract labour – as the productive activity of the proletariat – is merely a function of the system, rather than a choice or position on the part of the subjectivity of the working class. Kicillof and Starosta critique the manner in which class struggle theories of value reify the 'free consciousness of the wage labourer' as a 'natural attribute of human beings', where it is in fact 'the product of the commodity form itself'. Capitalism becomes, in this rendition, the 'imposition of the commodity form upon an abstractly free subjectivity'. This subjectivity is treated as if it exists both independently of and antecedent to the valorization process, when it is from this perspective an outcome of the latter. On these grounds, Kicillof and Starosta indict class struggle theories of value for their '*ontologisation* of the class struggle', which misses its historical specificity as a 'form of social being', and therefore as a social phenomenon. The antagonism is, instead, presented as one between 'two distinct existential logics', championing concrete labour as 'human doing', with the implication that it provides a counterpoint to abstract labour, or a natural principle upon which the latter is imposed in the name of value. With concrete labour is associated a working-class subjectivity with the capacity to act as a revolutionary force within capitalism. However, for its critics, any ontologization of class struggle insufficiently reckons with the way in which 'working-class subjectivity' is *socially determined* itself by the value form and its constitution.[72]

In this way, class struggle theories of value articulate resistance in and against social mediation by means of an 'abstractly free and self-determined' revolutionary subject similar in many respects to that proposed by traditional Marxism, somehow capable of escaping its determination as what is merely another alienated personification of economic categories. This mistakenly sees, in the 'personal freedom of personifications of commodities', the possibility of an unmediated and unalienated freedom.[73] Capitalists and workers are in this sense 'owners of commodities', rather than representatives of two contrasting existential logics. The capitalist wishes to receive the greatest possible return on their purchase of labour power by extending and intensifying the working day; in so doing, the capitalist expresses not their personality or subjectivity as such, but rather a compulsion instilled by the competitive struggle with other capitalists. The worker resists the extension and intensification of the working day because they desire the ability to be able to reproduce their labour power so that they can secure the full return upon their capabilities over the course of the day, week and working lifetime. The optimum means by which such security can be achieved is through the collaboration of the worker with their fellow workers, and the subsequent consolidation of class interests.[74] Thus, both sides of the equation act out personifications of economic categories that are socially determined, rather than ontological matters of fact. Indeed, the resistance of the worker against the duress of the labour process is not a manifestation of an antagonistic will or subjectivity *external* to the logic of the capitalist mode of production, but rather fully part and parcel of it.[75] The 'human content' that open and autonomist Marxism seeks to set free from its mediation as abstract labour has no subjectivity independent of its own alienation, as it is itself a socially mediated form of the development of capital. Thus, its pursuit chases an impossible relationship of 'false immediacy'.[76]

On the basis of such a critique, any subjectivity capable of overturning the rule of value would not exist external to capitalist social mediation, but would rather represent a development of the alienation of the seller of labour power as a commodity owner in the market, freed in a double sense by the process of primitive accumulation in which capitalist society is constituted. From this perspective, no unmediated or unalienated existence lies beyond the value form, but only the further progression of that mediation and alienation in a new and possibly – but not inevitably – more favourable guise. From the perspective of Starosta's 'practical criticism', abstract labour is not something historically specific to capitalism, but a transhistorical category in every society given expression in the objectified separation of products from their producers – a condition made possible by the particularity of the human capacity to conceive and execute, which, according to Marx, sets us apart from other animals.[77] It is, therefore, insufficient to simply pose against value a 'simple and unmediated' form of 'human doing' or 'sensuous human practice' resistant to the shape such objectifications assume in the value form. Any alternative must first recognize the intractability of contradiction and the impossibility of an unmediated life, whether within or beyond the rule of value.

6
Value in Crisis

In the previous chapter, we critically examined how an autonomist 'class struggle theory of value' is underpinned by the presentation of working-class subjectivity as consisting prior to the capitalist law of value.[1] In the wider autonomist tradition, this idea serves as the basis for the ascription to workers of a 'capacity and power of "auto-valorization"' independent of capitalist frameworks of control, command and measurement.[2] Here, value is something created autonomously by labour, and then subsequently subject to attempted capture and measure by capital. As we shall see in this closing chapter, this has consequences for how the concept of value is used to comprehend the possibility and actuality of capitalist crisis. Specifically, we will consider here the influential and invigorating theoretical contribution of the *postoperaist* tendency that springs from autonomist Marxism, whose most notable representatives are Antonio Negri and Michael Hardt.[3] Through this conceptual lens, we will consider whether the law of value is called into question by foregoing tendencies in the world of work, technology and economic life, and some of the innovative understandings of value that have begun to develop in order to understand these shifts. We will take finance as a case study of the potential crisis posed to value by the conditions of contemporary capitalist production, and how this is overcome. Surveying claims that the rule of value has entered into a 'crisis of measurability' owing to the hegemonic character within capitalist society of immaterial goods and services and the immaterial labour that produces them, the final part of this closing chapter considers the future of value and its critical understanding in a changing world.[4] We argue that, despite the apparent crisis of measurability that postoperaists theorize, value remains an important site of social and political struggle, the lifeblood of a capitalist system far from its final breakdown.

A Crisis of Value?

For postoperaists, contemporary capitalism is characterized by a crisis in the law of value which places value beyond measure, synonymous with the transformation of capitalism into another kind of system altogether.[5] As yet another instance of where select portions of Marx are brought to bear on the question of value, advocates of such a vision typically cite the authority of an unpublished section of the *Grundrisse*, Marx's notebooks for *Capital*, called the 'Fragment on Machines'.[6] Here, Marx hypothesized that capitalist dynamism would create a knowledge-intensive form of production based on the development of human capacities freed up from direct labour by the application of technology. Under the basically substantialist logic within which his work still sat at that point, the labour-time invested in work and the value produced, Marx proposed, would exceed the capacity of capitalist forms of measure and valuation to capture them. This would create an inevitable tendency towards the socialization of production, eventually making possible a postcapitalist society born within the shell of the old. Whilst Marx saw this as very much a distant possibility, and followed it up nowhere in his published work, the work of Negri and other postoperaists gained momentum in the 1990s by reading into real empirical trends in the rise of the 'New Economy' all the conditions for this to be happening in the here and now. For them, the future of value, then and now, is one of both crisis and radical transformation.

This prognosis has been taken forward to argue that, 'when confronting social production' – in other words, the cooperative, communicative and cognitive production characteristic of contemporary capitalism – 'capital is no longer able to measure value adequately, at least not in the

way it had previously'.[7] Productive activity is spontaneously cooperative and not organized through any capitalist
command or control.[8] The unmanaged and unmanageable
quality of contemporary labour creates the conditions for
a crisis in capital's capacity to measure and value economic
activity, because 'the wealth it creates is not (or is no longer)
measurable. How do you measure the value of knowledge, or
information, or a relationship of care and trust, or the basic
results of education or health services?' This immeasurability
concerns how 'divisions of the working day are breaking
down as work-time and life-time are increasingly mixed'
in an age of flexible work and handheld technologies. The
'capture of value tends to extend to envelop all the time of
life', with attendant consequences on the ability of money to
express this expanse of productive labour.[9]

In this way, and in common with some of the approaches
considered in the previous chapter, scholars working in the
postoperaist tradition correctly argue that a broader set of
activities that produce value within the contemporary circuits
of capitalism should be included in the understanding of
how the workplace relates to the economy at large, beyond
the 'restrictive conception of labour that dominates Marxist
analyses and focuses on paid employment in for-profit firms
and other organizations'. In this sense, postoperaismo 'extends
Marxist organizational analysis beyond traditional labour
processes' and 'enables an expanded focus on labour that
moves Marxist analyses away from the point of production
on the factory shop-floor – the "hidden abode" of classical
Marxism' – to place an expanded focus upon the production
of value at other points of social and economic activity.[10]

Drawing from this wellspring of external knowledge,
affect and creativity, contemporary production processes are
unlike industrial and agricultural processes and their outputs.
These were valued, 'however imperfectly', in previous modes
of capitalist accumulation based on the objectification of
collective know-how in formalized and standardized working
practices. Meanwhile, 'social products' such as cultural and
ideational works 'resist calculation' because they inhabit
a 'commons' of knowledge and affect that is unenclosable
within the confines of private property, and beyond capital's
capacity to manage and quantify it. Value production 'no

longer takes place primarily within the walls of the factory' but 'across the entire social terrain', immeasurable through conventional means.[11]

At the same time, labour itself within the production process attains a social character. Whereas the autonomist 'class struggle theory of value' encountered in the previous chapter saw the dual character of labour as simultaneously concrete and abstract constituting a permanent terrain of conflict within the labour process, for postoperaists this practical coexistence of concrete and abstract is the result of a more novel and recent state of affairs, whereby information technologies and the immaterial and affective quality of labour based in care, communication and creativity render labour 'immediately abstract', rather than abstract only after the fact through the exchange of its products. This immediate abstraction brings to a climax the progressive stripping away of work's specificity and particularity experienced in previous processes of deskilling and standardization in the workplace.[12] Through this immediate abstraction, labour attains a directly – rather than indirectly – social character, not through the exchange of the products of private labour in the market, but *within* the labour process owing to the social quality of the activities performed. The socialization of knowledge characterizing work in the New Economy is not managed or organized inside the workplace, but externally coordinated and spontaneous, posing a challenge for the measure and capture of the value it produces.

* * * *

Inspired by this theorization of value in contemporary capitalism, the 'question of measure' has become an issue of 'hot debate' amongst critical scholars of organization, playing out in a rich stream of empirical and theoretical work and popular academic writings proliferating around the postcapitalist potentialities unleashed by the crises sparked by new business models and technologies.[13] In a good example of the empirical application of postoperaist notions of value in organizational scholarship, Hugh Willmott proposes to 'situat[e] the creation and valorization of brand equity within the "full circuit of capital"', conceiving it as 'a form of co-production occurring in the sphere of circulation (as well as production)'. In this sense, whereas

> proponents of classical theory, and especially Marxian critique of political economy, relate the creation of value to the exercise of human labour power ... from a post-Marxian [or postoperaist] stance, attentiveness to value creation extends to the sphere of circulation where the labour of unwaged user-consumers is seen to participate in providing the content, and thereby to building the brand equity, of such businesses.[14]

Thus, focus falls on 'the forms of value-productive activity – such as the co-production of the symbolic values that comprise brand equity – that occur outside of an employment relationship'.[15] In this way, postoperaist conceptualizations of value also resonate with some of the emergent trends of the platform economy. Scholars working within the tradition have argued that the increasing amount of work occurring through digital platforms challenges the classical understanding of Marxism of waged labour as the only source of value. Whilst 'this activity has traditionally not been understood as labour', the business models of firms like Facebook can be seen to depend on 'the "free labour" of users', the platform profiting by organizing 'the activities of its users to turn them into productive labour' resulting in value. The argument runs that platforms such as Facebook capture 'sociality', manage it and make it productive. The 'free activity of communication is in fact a form of "free labour"' – in other words, 'capital's attempt to valorize social labour'.[16] The contemporary capitalist organization of production is structured so as to fulfil the primary purpose of capturing the value produced in society at large. In this respect, such 'crowdsourcing' Web 2.0 phenomena as Facebook and Google represent the 'the totality of linguistic machines' that act in society at large to capture 'the totality of sociality, emotions, desires, relational capacity [and] free labor'. These 'linguistic machines' have the effect of extending the working day with their acquisitive search for value.[17]

In tandem with these tendencies, the familiar characteristics of the commodity are thrown into flux. The intangible
products of immaterial labour 'pose a problem because
the methods of economic analysis generally rely on quantitative measures and calculate the value of objects that can
be counted, such as cars, computers and tons of wheat'.
In light of this, postoperaists question the validity of the
approach to value exhibited in orthodox Marxism, throwing
a simple quantitative appreciation of the working day into
relief against the infinitude of immaterial labour conducted
in cyber-time. Immaterial products 'tend to *exceed* all
quantitative measurement and take *common* forms', which
are thus harder to value.[18] Thus, the production of 'social
relations' is much harder to quantify than the production of
material goods, juxtaposing the latter 'traditional goods' with
what are labelled 'fictitious commodities'.[19] These conditions
combine to produce what postoperaists see as a growing
value crisis.

Finance and Value

Thus, this confrontation between spontaneously cooperative
labour uncoordinated by capitalist command and firms'
attempts to capture the resulting plenitude of value after
the fact produces a measurability crisis for which the only
solution, postoperaists argue, is recourse to the infrastructures of measurement and valuation afforded by the financial
markets. In earlier, more optimistic contributions such as
Empire, Hardt and Negri argued that immaterial labour and
its products have attained a hegemonic quality in contemporary capitalism and that the difficulty of quantifying and
valuing outputs poses not just a problem for individual organizations and actors, but for capitalism itself, potentiating an
immanent transformation into a new postcapitalist society.[20]
Their most recent work, *Assembly*, represents something of
a stepchange, with Hardt and Negri distancing themselves
from the claim that 'overflowing productive forces and the
immeasurable values of the common sound the death knell
of capital'.[21] Emphasis instead falls upon how financial and
technological developments 'domesticate immeasurability'

and 'stamp values on the immeasurable'. Specifically, Hardt and Negri identify derivatives as a means of this domestication. Hardt and Negri see in the rise of financialization an explanation for how measure persists in the face of this crisis, with derivatives 'form[ing] a complex web of conversions among a wide range of forms of wealth'.[22] This centres on the rise of intangibles in both requiring, and helping to construct, a new system of measuring value through financialized means:

> This value crisis is visible, among many things, in the rapidly growing share of intangibles to company valuation. Intangibles are per definition resources that fall outside of established accounting standards. This does of course not mean that there are no attempts to measure such intangible efforts. On the contrary there is a whole measurement industry that proposes more or less realistic models for the estimation of things like brand value or intellectual capital ... The quality of relations ... is the source of value in these practices or assets, whether it be the quality of a service encounter or the quality of relations between a brand and its stakeholders ... At the same time, however, a radically different way of conceiving of (and eventually measuring) value is emerging.[23]

Indeed, from the dot.com boom and bust onwards, postoperaists have been preoccupied with financialization as an extension of the widespread attempts on the part of capital to capture the immeasurable value produced by the immaterial, expansive cooperative and communicative labour of the digital, decentred workplace.[24] For postoperaismo, the financial infrastructure is the only institution sufficiently adaptable and fluid to operate within the similarly flexible and elusive logic of the new means of creating value through decentred and extended labour-time. Financialization coheres with, and brings under a degree of mathematical control, the economically immeasurable value cultivated with the new immaterial production.[25] These financialized modes of capturing and expressing the inscrutable and expansive value of new forms of economic activity in the New Economy

– digital, creative, relational – enable so-called 'immaterial' production to generate an 'economy of increasing returns' through the 'putting to work of the language of social relations, the activation of productive cooperation beyond the factory gate' and the extension of the working day through the blurring of life and leisure, 'respond[ing] to declining profit rates by intensifying the exploitation of the communicative–relational cooperation of the workforce'.[26]

What renders the financial markets so well suited to this new mode of production, postoperaists argue, is the willing and exuberant embrace of its ephemerality and fictitiousness. The purported crisis of measurability presents itself as an opportunity to the markets. The markets help bring order to the swelling and fluid mass of immaterial production conducted in the social sphere, rationalizing fictitious commodities in a formal set of figures that are themselves similarly fictitious. In this way, the 'collective intelligence' at the heart of the new production 'escapes any objective measurement' – the attempts at which in the arena of finance existing only as extravagant illusions. The value of this collective intelligence is 'the subjective expression of the expectation for future profits effectuated by financial markets who procure themselves rent in this way'.[27] The self-referential and subjective attribution of market values to anticipated future profit provides some form of measure to a production process founded upon immeasurable quantities of unpaid labour-time, such that its 'exploitation and expropriation' of cooperative labour finds 'immediate valorization on the markets'.[28] This is because markets render interpretable a 'process of valorization ... not immediately computable at the time of production'. In this way, financialization is characterized as an integrated part of these processes, 'spread[ing] across the entire economic cycle, co-existing with it'. Finance is thus '*consubstantial* to the very production of goods and services', with immaterial labour and its subjective, self-referential valuation in the financial markets sharing the same productive deployment of communication and language in creating value.[29]

In this last respect, referring to how the New Economy 'dot.com bubble' was boosted by the likes of Alan Greenspan setting out 'conventions' upon which investors then acted,

Christian Marazzi posits that the functioning of markets and of successful investments is not governed by the correct actions with regard to underlying rates of profit and so on, but by the endlessly self-referential collective rumour and recommendation of the wider herd of market players and investors, including the media and figures in financial governance.[30] As such, investors look not to what they think *they* should do, but rather to what they think *others* will do. Such processes rely on the new forms of co-optation in contemporary capitalism of communication and linguistic capability. Performative utterances are *productive* of 'real facts', whether or not there is a material basis. This is what allows the values of stock exchange securities to 'make reference to themselves and not their underlying economic value'.[31] This tendency is one that afflicts money itself, which 'has finally been completely dematerialized: it has become pure *money-sign*. Its measurement is thus conventional.'[32] However, just because share values exist only at the level of language and communication, without material referent, does not necessarily entail that their impact is not felt materially. In a world in which linguistic production structures every institution, the 'linguistic–communicative act is constitutive of the money, the marriage, and even of the enterprise, of which the shares ... purchased represent a portion of the share capital that allows the company to function economically'.[33]

For the postoperaists, this economy of sign and symbol accommodates to the character of contemporary capitalism, in which what is produced is immaterial, and a general 'readability crisis' on the part of capital affects its 'capacity to read the composition of labor on whose exploitation it depends'.[34] Indeed, for postoperaists, there is nothing at all 'fictitious' about the capital represented in share prices fostered by the conventional wisdom of investors. Rather, these prices are the expression of an intangible and immaterial form of production whose value is effectively beyond measure, but which finds a degree of reconciliation in the symbolic and communicative content of the share price. Postoperaists see stock prices not as 'the reflection of the irrational exuberance of speculation', but, instead, as representing 'the real growth in social production' and the time that it occupies.[35]

In drawing a link between how value is produced and its expression in the financial markets, postoperaists do not appear to indulge the left-populist distinction between a productive 'real' economy sustained on a material productive base and a 'false' financial economy, unproductive and completely uprooted from production. One might infer from their work on the dot.com boom and the 2008 financial crash that financialization is not an unproductive or parasitic deviation, cooked up through a conspiratorial project of deliberate economic distortion instigated by greedy financiers or neoliberal intellectuals, as in some misguided populist appraisals of the rise of finance. Rather, it is the form of capital accumulation symmetrical with new processes of value production – a result and function of underlying and ongoing shifts in the constitution of society's productive processes towards working practices characterized by a wealth of free labour dispersed into society at large and recouped by digital infrastructures as an immeasurable plenitude of value.[36] This has obvious benefits over some of the boundary policing around productive and unproductive sectors of the economy found in other approaches covered in this book.

However, as time has passed, the function of finance as a kind of rent-extraction mechanism for not only the measure but the appropriation of value from spontaneous cooperative forms of production has become a stronger theme of postoperaist writing on the future of value. Whilst the 'subsumption of the common' that fuels these financial processes was once taken to express the interconnection between finance and the deepest fabric of human cognition and sociality engaged in the new forms of production, it is recast in recent work by Hardt and Negri as a relationship of external predation upon a previously untouched productive harmony.[37] A substantialist, Smithian understanding underpins recent critiques of how financialized streams of speculation and valuation 'extract value' from the hard-to-capture expanse of value 'buried in the earth and ... embedded in society', as if value lies within things awaiting discovery.[38] In this way, for postoperaists, rent has replaced profit as the key means of revenue-raising in contemporary capitalism.[39] Finance is now posed as a parasitical force extracting from a naturalistic productive sphere of unbridled creativity that, if left alone, would function of its own accord.

The Future of Value

Setting aside the 'becoming rent of profit', for postoperaists only the financial markets possess the elusive capacity to quantify what is immeasurable, expressing the growth in social production and temporarily suspending the crisis of value. But for the other readings of Marx's value theory discussed in this book, the battle to bring measure is always present in production itself, precisely because of how the organization of labour is subordinated to the logics of the valorization process as a whole, and the market mediation of its products as commodities exchanged by means of money. The postoperaist recognition of the capacity of finance to convert and equalize values in such a way as to suspend the measurability crisis does touch upon this monetary character of value in capitalist society and the role of market-mediation in establishing its measure. But monetary and financial logics intertwine with production more closely than postoperaists would attest – and arguably intertwine already in the workplace. The financial derivatives Hardt and Negri eulogize do not bring measure to or extract from a pre-existing plenitude of value, but rather represent a monetary process validating inscrutable activities as value-producing. In this respect, we can locate it in the interface between the valorization process and the labour process we have explored in previous chapters, and namely in the concept of socially necessary labour time.

Rather than being restricted to the finance sector alone, then, the 'conversion' and equalization of labours and the value they produce still proceeds in working environments characterized by conditions of 'immaterial labour', confronting measure not as a crisis, but as what we might better conceive as a *challenge*. Specifically, the crisis is overcome through the articulation of the relationship between what goes on in the workplace and its mediation in the market – in other words, 'socially necessary labour-time' (SNLT, see chapter 2 and chapter 5). Postoperaists claim that SNLT is no longer the relevant measure for value in the conditions of immateriality characterizing labour in contemporary capitalist society, with shifts in the qualitative and quantitative character of labour in the contemporary economy having rendered 'the relation between time and quantity of produced value' highly 'difficult to determine'.[40] But from an autonomist perspective based on the 'struggle' theory of value presented in the previous chapter, Massimo De Angelis and David Harvie empirically apply the understanding of SNLT to the empirical example of how higher education institutions measure 'immaterial labour' through new metrics and standards.[41] They refute the postoperaist 'celebration' of the immeasurability of 'immaterial, self-organised and cooperative production' and the redundancy of the law of value, highlighting instead how the 'war of measure' typifying Taylorism continues in knowledge intensive work through the imposition of what they call 'diachronic' and 'synchronic' processes of measuring SNLT.[42] The first drives down the 'labour-time socially-necessary for the "production" of ideas' through the pursuit of efficiencies and standards. The second commensurates heterogenous activities – both internally and externally – by abstracting from the specificities of academic labour 'benchmarks and norms' such as journal ratings, and rankings and accreditation of courses and modules. This 'constructs' SNLT in line with expectations external, rather than intrinsic, to the 'immaterial doings' of the labour – the form it assumes in the market shaping its content.[43]

The example of how new benchmarks and metrics have been imposed on immaterial labour in the higher education sector highlights the potential applicability of more conventional ways of overcoming the problem – if not the crisis – of measurability. Undoubtedly, this labour differs from the 'material' factory labour of Marx's own time, but it is still measured. It is just one example of how the idea of the measurability crisis 'does not seem to refer to what billions of people across the planet do every day under the surveillance of bosses vitally concerned about how much time the workers are at their job and how well they do it'.[44] Whilst postoperaists might see the contemporary conditions of production in capitalist organizing as rendering impossible the capacity of firms to measure the value they create, 'capitalist organizations, aided by the heirs of Frederick Winslow Taylor are doing just that'.[45] The persistence of these measures reveals not a crisis of value but, thus, rather a *problem* the continuities of the capitalist valorization process prove more than capable of confronting and overcoming.

* * * *

Considering the importance of immaterial labour to their account of the present and future of value in a world of crisis and transformation, Hardt and Negri take a surprisingly materialist approach to value. Ironically, then, the value theory seemingly most attuned to the future of value is also one that brings us full circle, back to some of the substance theories of value we encountered in the first chapter. On one hand, Hardt and Negri's extension of the theorization of value beyond production alone to encapsulate 'the total cycle of capital' improves on the orthodox Marxist preoccupation with production at the expense of how moments of consumption and circulation also determine value.[46] But, simply extending the moment of production beyond the factory walls to fill social life itself, at base Hardt and Negri retain a substantialist understanding of value closer to Ricardo's labour theory of value than Marx's 'value theory of labour', for which the aim lay 'less in its explanatory power to describe the causal determination of prices than in recognizing that exchange value is a social abstraction'.[47] Labour – for Hardt and Negri, as for the most traditional Marxism – is still 'the source of wealth in capitalist society', and any changes in its immediate content impact upon capitalism's capacity to measure its value, without any recognition of the layers of social mediation that lie between concrete labour and its eventual abstraction in value.[48]

This simply repeats the flaws of the substantialist understanding of value we encountered in chapter 1. Situating value in the amount of labour expended in a commodity's production implies that the commodity produced by the most 'unskilful and lazy' worker would have the most value.[49] The labour-time that determines value is instead that validated as socially necessary through the exchange of its products in the market. What is distinctive is not concrete labour's immediate content but its formal mediation as abstract labour, both premonitorily in production and finally in exchange. In Hardt and Negri's ultimately productivist account of the 'immediately abstract' character of contemporary labour, the valorization process plays no part in rendering private labours social inside and outside production – they are always-already social, immune from the social mediation of their measure in the workplace and the marketplace.[50] Hardt and Negri scale up changes in the immediate character and content of labour to claims about changes in capitalism itself – even where features of the valorization process, of which the labour process is just a carrier, maintain an underlying continuity of form and function.[51]

Thus, despite calling into question the capacity to measure value, postoperaist approaches have much in common with traditional applications of Marxian value theory to the study of work and economic life. They focus myopically on labour and production as the central sites of both inquiry and contention within the capitalist circuit and the determination of value. The postoperaists – somewhat counterintuitively, considering their otherwise anti-productivist credentials – place production at the very foundation of wealth creation, and apply this principal to financialization in turn. This has some benefits, avoiding crude differentiations between productive and unproductive economic activities, as we have seen, but also contains a denied productivism that centres the workplace as the locus of all change and meaning in capitalist society – albeit it on an expanded basis.[52] Just as with other stripes of productivism, changes in capitalism and the capacity to produce and capture value are extrapolated from changes in the immediate content taken by labour within production. But the perspectives advanced in this book from more relational and 'struggle'-oriented readings of value broaden this focus and make for a perspective much more circumspect about the possibility of reading off wider changes when the essential social forms of capitalist society carry over independent of changes in the way value is produced. Value persists, by hook or by crook, because it is constituted apart from production. As Moishe Postone points out, there is a common perspective uniting, on one hand, those who 'maintain that the labor theory of value had been valid in the past', but not today, and, on the other hand, those who maintain an attachment to the traditional labour theory of value that 'reduce[s] everything to the amount of labor-time ... that went into it'. In neither is value seen as something more than production, as a 'historically specific form of wealth', determined and constituted in society as a whole.[53]

The 'form analysis' advocated in this book, meanwhile, exposes the true qualitative sociological significance of the value theory we can reconstruct from Marx. Without forgoing the study of production, it opens out upon an expansive terrain of social and political contestation and critique that shows us how a fixation on labour alone is insufficient to grasp what really makes value tick as part of a historically specific mode of organizing production and exchange. Moreover, labour alone cannot constitute a basis on which either to rule out or rule in epochal shifts in the character of value. The new readings of Marx presented here therefore trump analyses, such as that of the postoperaists, that narrowly restrict themselves to the sphere of production, missing the social relations that foreground labour and the social forms assumed by its results. The new readings of Marx also circumvent the pitfall of seeing 'free labour' everywhere, collapsing the distinction between production and circulation, and in so doing erasing any sense of the determination of labour as wage labour. This, we might suggest, leads either to reducing the analysis or to expanding it to breaking point. Value, far from being in crisis or beyond measure, is a persistent part of social and political life in capitalist society, within and against which we struggle daily as a matter of survival and subsistence.

* * * *

Here the study of value opens out upon the question of alternatives, however hard they are to perceive at the present time. Marx 'thought that the demand to abolish the calculation of value was realisable, although of course only when commodity production, that is, the production of independent individuals for the market, is abolished. This demand is a compelling consequence, a substantial and not merely an accidental component of Marx's theory of value.'[54] Rather than an impossible immediacy, value as a historically specific form of mediation always contains the unfulfilled possibility of its radical de- and re-mediation because it mediates, at its core, the capital–labour relation which is, by its very nature, characterized by struggle, and thus unstable.[55] And, vice versa, as the class struggle theory of value outlined in the previous chapter showed us, value 'mediates the existence of antagonisms as a condition of [its] own existence'. In this way, capitalism's forms of mediation, value included, are antagonistic top to bottom, and antagonisms and the forms in which they are temporarily suspended or resolved are themselves always mediated. The question is one of which mediations, and whether they are better or worse than the ones we have to hand right now.

Thus, whilst ultimately pessimistic and with no easy answers or revolutionary schemes, the reconstruction of the critique of political economy presented in this book provides some basis to consider new realistic and realizable forms of mediation – new objectifications of human practical activity that, whilst unable to escape value completely, offer piecemeal ways to make life more bearable and fulfilled in, against and beyond it. It directs our attention away from the workplace as the sole locus in and through which social change can be organized. The search for alternatives need not here be reduced to different ways of organizing production or escaping work, for instance. Situating value at the articulation point of production and exchange opens out upon a wide array of struggles, not only around production but around consumption and circulation as well – a break with the productivism of the classical tradition, orthodox Marxism and, arguably, the populist politics of our own time.

Indeed, in the context of such a populist politics, the topic, if not the theory, of value will only grow more fraught, and become more urgent, in the years to come. In the face of the contemporary technological changes on which the postoperaists optimistically focus, as well as the prevailing moral panic about automation quite literally coming down the assembly line, the populist assertion of productive identities associated with the perceived capacity of groups and individuals to lay claim to the status and rewards of value productiveness is a response to a moving situation in which the certainties attached to industrial labour are fast degrading. Hence, the politics of productivism takes increasingly volatile directions, lashing out at a succession of unproductive outsiders.

In this respect, the rise of populism has been associated widely with industrial and labour market change, including the substitution of human labour with technology, typically in communities and locales once characterized by a high proportion of manufacturing jobs. Attributed to the 'left behind', populism is viewed as an expression of alienation and anomie in the wake of the loss of well-paying, skilled jobs in working-class areas, and the apportionment of blame for these changes upon various 'others'. These 'others' are typically posed as outside forces threatening the nation or locality in a parasitic or conspiratorial way: migrants, global institutions, bankers, etc. Complex material and political forces are condensed into explanations that identify personalized culprits for the industrial or economic malaise experienced by the nation and its people.

But there are significant implications of the heavily automated and AI-driven terrain of so-called 'Industry 4.0' for the capacity of current and future workers to stake productivist claims to a productive identity, based upon one's contribution to the local, national or economic 'value' of production. With these tendencies, the basis for previous claims to a virtuous productive identity – say, a labour theory of value whereby all wealth was that produced by the workers, to whom it should be rightly returned – is also fading from view, with human labour augmented by technology, and robots seen as a threat rather than themselves a part of the 'wealth' produced by workers. This may have the consequence of creating new forms of expression of dissent and dissatisfaction that may be even more dangerous or nihilistic than the productivisms of the past.

Rather than a topic of dry academic debate, then, value is still very much up for grabs. At their best, the theories gathered here reveal how we subsist and socially reproduce not only ourselves and others, but society itself *in and against* the form of value. Whether there is anything *beyond* value, however, is a question to which there presently seems no easy theoretical or practical answer. For the 'new readings' of Marx surveyed here, 'we all produce society' – through time, across places – 'but we do this in certain forms'.[56] The productive activities of a given society, taken by themselves, are insufficient to understand it. Rather, the forms and purposes under which this productive activity takes place, which shape its practice and experience, are key.[57] Freed of the boundary work of policing who is productive and unproductive, the politics of value comes down to the investigation and contestation of these forms and purposes through which the world of work and economic life is made and remade, today and in the future.

Notes

Introduction

1 W. Bonefeld, 2014. *Critical Theory and the Critique of Political Economy: On Subversion and Negative Reason*. London: Bloomsbury; R. Bellofiore and T. R. Riva, 2015. The Neue Marx-Lekture: Putting the Critique of Political Economy Back into the Critique of Society. *Radical Philosophy*, 189, pp. 24–36; F. H. Pitts, 2015. The Critique of Political Economy as a Critical Social Theory. *Capital & Class*, 39(3), pp. 537–45.

2 M. Horkheimer, 1976 [1937]. Traditional and Critical Theory. In P. Connerton (ed.), *Critical Sociology*. London: Penguin, pp. 206–24.

3 P. Mirowski, 1991. Postmodernism and the Social Theory of Value. *Journal of Post Keynesian Economics*, 13(4), pp. 565–82 (p. 578); P. Mirowski, 1989. *More Heat than Light: Economics as Social Physics, Physics as Nature's Economics*. Cambridge University Press, p. 265.

4 M. Mazzucato, 2019. *The Value of Everything: Making and Taking in the Global Economy*. London: Penguin, p. 7.

5 Mazzucato 2019, p. 8.

6 Mazzucato 2019, pp. 7, 22.

7 R. L. Heilbroner, 1983. The Problem of Value in the Constitution of Economic Thought. *Social Research*, 50(2), pp. 253–77 (pp. 253–6).

8 Aristotle, 2000. *The Politics*. Trans. T. A. Sinclair. London: Penguin; Aristotle, 2004. *Nicomachean Ethics*. Trans. J. A. K. Thompson. London: Penguin; Mirowski 1989, p. 145; A. Monroe, ed., 1924. *Early Economic Thought*. Cambridge, MA: Harvard University Press, p. 27.

9 A. Dinerstein and M. Neary, 2002. From Here to Utopia: Finding Inspiration for the Labour Debate. In A. Dinerstein and

M. Neary (eds.), *The Labour Debate: An Investigation into the Theory and Reality of Capitalist Work*. Aldershot: Ashgate, pp. 1–26 (p. 13).

10 Heilbroner 1983, pp. 253–6; Mirowski 1989.

1 Value as Substance

1 R. L. Heilbroner, 1983. The Problem of Value in the Constitution of Economic Thought. *Social Research*, 50(2), pp. 253–77 (p. 259).

2 P. Mirowski, 1989. *More Heat than Light: Economics as Social Physics, Physics as Nature's Economics*. Cambridge University Press, pp. 192, 399.

3 Aristotle, 2000. *The Politics*. Trans. T. A. Sinclair. London: Penguin; Aristotle, 2004. *Nicomachean Ethics*. Trans. J. A. K. Thompson. London: Penguin; Mirowski 1989, p. 145; A. Monroe, ed. 1924. *Early Economic Thought*. Cambridge, MA: Harvard University Press, p. 27.

4 Mirowski 1989, p. 142.

5 P. Mirowski, 1990. Learning the Meaning of a Dollar: Conservation Principles and the Social Theory of Value in Economic Theory. *Social Research*, 57(3), pp. 689–717 (p. 697); Mirowski 1989, p. 142.

6 A. Smith, 1982. *The Wealth of Nations*. London: Penguin, p. 150, and D. Ricardo, 1981. *The Works and Correspondence of David Ricardo*. Vol I, ed. P. Sraffa and M. Dobb. Cambridge University Press; K. Marx, 1976. *Capital*. Vol. I. London: Penguin.

7 Mirowski 1989, p. 148. This section draws, in part, on the discussion in M. Bolton and F. H. Pitts, 2018. *Corbynism: A Critical Approach*. Bingley: Emerald, pp. 135–8.

0 M. Mazzucato, 2019. *The Value of Everything: Making and Taking in the Global Economy*. London: Penguin, p. 26.

9 Mirowski 1989, p. 148.

10 Mirowski 1989, pp. 159–60.

11 Mazzucato 2019, p. 28.

12 Mazzucato 2019, p. 33.

13 K. Marx, 1970. *Contribution to the Critique of Political Economy*. London: Lawrence and Wishart, pp. 54–5.

14 Marx 1970, pp. 55–7.

15 Mazzucato 2019, p. 33.

16 Mazzucato 2019, pp. 37–40.

17 Heilbroner 1983, p. 263.
18 Smith 1982, pp. 430–1.
19 Heilbroner 1983, pp. 263–4.
20 S. Clarke, 1991. *Marx, Marginalism and Modern Sociology.* London: Palgrave, pp. 21–8, 97–9; K. Marx, 1991. *Capital.* Vol. III. London: Penguin, pp. 953–70.
21 S. Veca, 1971. Value, Labor and the Critique of Political Economy. *Telos,* 1971(9), pp. 48–64 (p. 52).
22 Marx 1970, pp. 50, 57–8.
23 Veca 1971, pp. 48–52.
24 A. Dinerstein and M. Neary, 2002. From Here to Utopia: Finding Inspiration for the Labour Debate. In *The Labour Debate: An Investigation into the Theory and Reality of Capitalist Work.* Aldershot: Ashgate, pp. 1–26 (p. 13).
25 Veca 1971, pp. 48–52.
26 Marx 1970, p. 60.
27 Heilbroner 1983, pp. 264–5.
28 Heilbroner 1983, pp. 265–6.
29 F. H. Pitts, 2020. The Multitude and the Machine: Populism, Productivism, Posthumanism. *Political Quarterly,* 91(2), pp. 362–72; J. Cruddas and F. H. Pitts, 2020. The Politics of Postcapitalism: Labour and Our Digital Futures. *Political Quarterly,* 91(2), pp. 275–86.
30 Mazzucato 2019, pp. 41–5.
31 E. Wilson, 2003. To the Finland Station: A Study in the Writing and Acting of History. *New York Review of Books,* p. 291.
32 Dinerstein and Neary 2002, p. 24.
33 Heilbroner 1983, pp. 260–1.
34 T. Veblen, 1969. *The Place of Science in Modern Civilization and Other Essays.* New York: Capricorn Books, pp. 162, 280–1; see Mirowski 1989, p. 139.
35 Heilbroner 1983, pp. 260–1.
36 Ricardo 1981.
37 S. Himmelweit and S. Mohun, 1981. Real Abstractions and Anomalous Assumptions. In I. Steedman (ed.), *The Value Controversy.* London: New Left Books, pp. 224–65 (p. 245).
38 Himmelweit and Mohun 1981, pp. 253–4.
39 A. Saad-Filho, 1997. Concrete and Abstract Labour in Marx's Theory of Value. *Review of Political Economy,* 9(4), pp. 457–77 (pp. 466–8).
40 Mirowski 1989, pp. 177, 180.
41 Mirowski, 1989, p. 180.
42 Marx 1976; D. Elson, 1979. The Value Theory of Labour. In D.

Elson (ed.), *Value: The Representation of Labour in Capitalism.* London: CSE Books, pp. 115–80 (pp. 139–41); J. Holloway, 2015. Read Capital: The First Sentence of *Capital* Starts with Wealth, Not with the Commodity. *Historical Materialism,* 23(3), pp. 3–26.

43 Elson 1979, p. 124.

44 Marx, quoted in Elson 1979, p. 124.

45 Elson 1979, p. 123.

46 K. Marx, 1998. *The German Ideology.* New York: Prometheus Books; see Elson 1979, pp. 123–4.

47 Himmelweit and Mohun 1981, pp. 232–3.

48 M. Heinrich, 2012. *An Introduction to the Three Volumes of Karl Marx's* Capital. Trans. A. Locascio. New York: Monthly Review Press, p. 42.

49 Heilbroner 1983, pp. 266–7.

50 C. Arthur, 2013. The Practical Truth of Abstract Labour. In R. Bellofiore, G. Starosta and P. Thomas (eds.), *In Marx's Laboratory: Critical Interpretations of the Grundrisse.* Leiden: Brill, pp. 101–20.

51 J. B. Foster, 1999. Marx's Theory of Metabolic Rift: Classical Foundations for Environmental Sociology. *American Journal of Sociology,* 105(2), pp. 366–405; J. B. Foster, 2016. Marxism in the Anthropocene: Dialectical Rifts on the Left. *International Critical Thought,* 6(3), pp. 393–421.

52 Marx 1976, pp. 284–5.

53 F. H. Pitts, 2020. Creative Labour, Metabolic Rift and the Crisis of Social Reproduction. In M. Banks and K. Oakley (eds.), *Cultural Industries and the Environmental Crisis: New Approaches for Policy.* London: Palgrave Macmillan.

54 H. Gerstenberger, 2007. *Impersonal Power: History and Theory of the Bourgeois State.* Leiden and Boston: Brill; E. M. Wood, 1991. *The Pristine Culture of Capitalism: A Historical Essay on Old Regimes and Modern States.* London: Verso; E. M. Wood, 1995. *Democracy against Capitalism: Renewing Historical Materialism.* Cambridge University Press; E. M. Wood, 2002. *The Origin of Capitalism: A Longer View.* London: Verso; M. Bolton, 2019. Justice and the State Form: Conceptual History and the Separation of State and Society. Ph.D. thesis, Department of Humanities, University of Roehampton.

55 Marx 1976, p. 272.

56 S. Rioux, G. LeBaron and P. J. Verovšek, 2020. Capitalism and Unfree Labor: A Review of Marxist Perspectives on Modern Slavery. *Review of International Political Economy,* 27(3), pp.

709–31; see also S. M. Sorentino, 2019. Natural Slavery, Real Abstraction, and the Virtuality of Anti-Blackness. *Theory & Event*, 22(3), pp. 630–73; S. M. Sorentino, 2019. The Abstract Slave: Anti-Blackness and Marx's Method. *International Labor and Working-Class History*, 96, pp. 17–37.

57 C. Chen, 2013. The Limit Point of Capitalist Equality: Notes Toward an Abolitionist Antiracism. *Endnotes*, 3, pp. 202–23.

58 Marx, cited in J. Clegg, 2020. A Theory of Capitalist Slavery. *Journal of Historical Sociology*, 33(1), pp. 74–98 (p. 75).

59 B. Cooke, 2003. The Denial of Slavery in Management Studies. *Journal of Management Studies*, 40(8), pp. 1895–1918; J. Clegg, 2015. Capitalism and Slavery. *Critical Historical Studies*, 2(2), pp. 281–304.

60 F. Wilderson III, 2003. Gramsci's Black Marx: Whither the Slave in Civil Society? *Social Identities*, 9(2), pp. 225–40; S. Issar, 2020. Listening to Black Lives Matter: Racial Capitalism and the Critique of Neoliberalism. *Contemporary Political Theory*, DOI: 10.1057/s41296-020-00399-0.

61 Issar 2020; see also C. Robinson, 1983. *Black Marxism*. Chapel Hill: University of North Carolina Press; J. Melamed, 2015. Racial Capitalism. *Critical Ethnic Studies*, 1(1), pp. 76–85; H. White, 2020. How Is Capitalism Racial? Fanon, Critical Theory and the Fetish of Antiblackness. *Social Dynamics: A Journal of African Studies*, DOI: 10.1080/02533952.2020.1758871.

62 Marx 1976, p. 280.

63 Marx 1976, pp. 283–306.

64 The paragraphs that follow draw on F. H. Pitts, 2013. Labour-time in the Dot.Com Bubble: Marxist Approaches. *Fast Capitalism*, 10(1), pp. 145–57, and F. H. Pitts, 2015. Always Be Closing: Experiencing and Theorizing Time and Wage in a UK Call Center. *Tamara: Journal of Critical Organization Inquiry*, 13(4), pp. 39–48.

65 Marx 1976, pp. 178–9.

66 Marx 1976, pp. 340–1.

67 Marx 1976, pp. 300–1.

68 P. Thompson, 1989. *The Nature of Work: An Introduction to Debates on the Labour Process*. London: Macmillan.

69 Marx 1976, pp. 324–5.

70 Marx 1976, pp. 324–6, pp. 340–1.

71 Marx 1976, p. 646.

72 Marx 1976, p. 367.

73 Marx 1976, pp. 342–4.

74 Marx 1976, pp. 342–4.

75 Marx 1976, p. 344.
76 Marx 1976, p. 432.
77 Marx 1976, pp. 429–31.
78 Marx 1976, pp. 437–8.
79 See N. Geras, 1985. The Controversy about Marx and Justice. *New Left Review*, 150(3), pp. 47–85, for a discussion.
80 Marx 1976, pp. 130–1.
81 M. Heinrich, 2012. *An Introduction to the Three Volumes of Karl Marx's* Capital. Trans. A. Locascio. New York: Monthly Review Press, p. 43.
82 Marx 1970.
83 J. Baudrillard, 1973. *The Mirror of Production*. Trans. M. Poster. New York: Telos.
84 Baudrillard 1973, pp. 17–19.
85 M. Poster, 1973. Translator's Introduction. In J. Baudrillard, 1973. *The Mirror of Production*. Trans. M. Poster. New York: Telos, pp. 1–15 (p. 5).
86 M. Postone, 1993. *Time, Labor, and Social Domination: A Reinterpretation of Marx's Critical Theory*. Cambridge University Press.
87 Baudrillard 1973, pp. 22–3.
88 Baudrillard 1973, pp. 18–19.
89 H. Reichelt, 2005. Social Reality as Appearance: Some Notes on Marx's Conception of Reality. In W. Bonefeld and K. Psychopedis (eds.), *Human Dignity: Social Autonomy and the Critique of Capitalism*. Aldershot: Ashgate, pp. 31–68 (p. 63).
90 P. Murray, 2013. Unavoidable Crises: Reflections on Backhaus and the Development of Marx's Value-Form Theory in the *Grundrisse*. In R. Bellofiore, G. Starosta and P. Thomas (eds.), *In Marx's Laboratory: Critical Interpretations of the Grundrisse*. Leiden: Brill, pp. 121–46 (p. 130).
91 H.-G. Backhaus, 1980. On the Dialectics of the Value-Form. *Thesis Eleven*, 1, pp. 94–119 (p. 100).
92 M. Heinrich and X. Wei, 2012. The Interpretation of Capital: An Interview with Michael Heinrich. *World Review of Political Economy*, 2(4), pp. 708–28 (p. 722).
93 Quoted in Reichelt 2005, p. 52.

2 Value as Relation

1 P. Mirowski, 1989. *More Heat than Light: Economics as Social*

Physics, Physics as Nature's Economics. Cambridge University Press, p. 399.

2 Mirowski 1989, pp. 143–4; P. Mirowski, 1990. Learning the Meaning of a Dollar: Conservation Principles and the Social Theory of Value in Economic Theory. *Social Research*, 57(3), pp. 689–717 (p. 697).

3 K. Marx, 1976. *Capital*. Vol. I. London: Penguin, p. 151.

4 Aristotle, 2000. *The Politics*. Trans. T. A. Sinclair, London: Penguin; Aristotle, 2004. *Nicomachean Ethics*. Trans. J. A. K. Thompson. London: Penguin; Mirowski 1989, p. 145; A. Monroe, ed. 1924. *Early Economic Thought*. Cambridge, MA: Harvard University Press, p. 27.

5 H.-G. Backhaus, 1980. On the Dialectics of the Value-Form. *Thesis Eleven*, 1, pp. 94–119; R. Bellofiore, 2009. A Ghost Turning into a Vampire: The Concept of Capital and Living Labour. In R. Bellofiore and R. Fineschi (eds.), *Re-reading Marx: New Perspectives after the Critical Edition*. Basingstoke: Palgrave Macmillan, pp. 178–94; R. Bellofiore and T. R. Riva, 2015. The Neue Marx-Lekture: Putting the Critique of Political Economy Back into the Critique of Society. *Radical Philosophy*, 189, pp. 24–36; D. Elson, 1979. The Value Theory of Labour. In D. Elson (ed.), *Value: The Representation of Labour in Capitalism*. London: CSE Books, pp. 115–80; M. Heinrich, 2012. *An Introduction to the Three Volumes of Karl Marx's Capital*. Trans. A. Locascio. New York: Monthly Review Press; H. Reichelt, 2005. Social Reality as Appearance: Some Notes on Marx's Conception of Reality. In W. Bonefeld and K. Psychopedis (eds.), *Human Dignity: Social Autonomy and the Critique of Capitalism*. Aldershot: Ashgate, pp. 31–68.

6 J. Appleby, 1978. *Economic Thought and Ideology in Seventeenth-Century England*. Princeton University Press, pp. 179, 229; Mirowski 1989, pp. 150–3.

7 S. Bailey, 1967 [1825]. *Critical Dissertation on Value*. London: Cass, pp. 4–5.

8 Bailey 1967 [1825], pp. 24, 94; Mirowski 1989, pp. 187–8.

9 Bailey 1967 [1825], p. 96.

10 Mirowski 1989, p. 189.

11 Mirowski 1989, pp. 190–1, p. 400.

12 See J. Furner, 2004. Marx's Critique of Samuel Bailey. *Historical Materialism*, 12(2), pp. 89–110.

13 Elson 1979, p. 152.

14 K. Marx, 1971. *Theories of Surplus Value*. Vol. III. Moscow: Progress, p. 162; Mirowski 1989, p. 191.

15 Marx 1976, p. 141, n. 17.

16 M. M. Robertson and J. D. Wainwright, 2013. The Value of Nature to the State. *Annals of the Association of American Geographers*, 103(4), pp. 890–905 (p. 896).

17 K. Karatani, 2005. *Transcritique: On Kant and Marx*. Boston, MA: MIT Press, p. 5.

18 Robertson and Wainwright 2013, pp. 895–6, pp. 900–1.

19 Some passages in this chapter draw from material first published as F. H. Pitts, 2019. Value Form Theory, Open Marxism & the New Reading of Marx. In A. C. Dinerstein, A. G. Vela, E. González and J. Holloway (eds.), *Open Marxism IV: Against a Closing World*. London: Pluto Press. Thanks to David Castle and the publishers for permission to reuse.

20 M. Heinrich, 2017. 'Capital' after MEGA: Discontinuities, Interruptions, and New Beginnings. *Crisis and Critique*, 3(3), pp. 93–138 (p. 136).

21 F. H. Pitts, 2017. *Critiquing Capitalism Today: New Ways to Read Marx*. New York: Palgrave.

22 Elson 1979.

23 Mirowski 1989, p. 191.

24 Mirowski 1989, pp. 201–2.

25 Mirowski 1989, p. 183.

26 Mirowski 1989, pp. 201–2.

27 W. C Roberts, 2017. The Value of *Capital*. *Jacobin*, 27 March: www.jacobinmag.com/2017/03/marxs-inferno-capital-david-harvey-response.

28 M. Mazzucato, 2019. *The Value of Everything: Making and Taking in the Global Economy*. London: Penguin, p. 34.

29 R. L. Heilbroner, 1983. The Problem of Value in the Constitution of Economic Thought. *Social Research*, 50(2), pp. 253–77 (p. 267). Among Marx's critics, an exception Heilbroner singles out is P. Samuelson, 1976. *Economics*. 10th edn. New York: McGraw Hill.

30 M. Heinrich and X. Wei, 2012. The Interpretation of Capital: An Interview with Michael Heinrich. *World Review of Political Economy*, 2(4), pp. 708–28 (p. 725).

31 I. I. Rubin, 1975. *Essays on Marx's Theory of Value*. Montreal: Black Rose Books, pp. 96–7.

32 Backhaus 1980, pp. 94–119.

33 A. Aumeeruddy and R. Tortajada, 1979. Reading Marx on Value: A Note on the Basic Texts. In D. Elson (ed.), *Value: The Representation of Labour in Capitalism*. London: CSE Books, pp. 1–13 (p. 3).

34 G. Kay, 1979. Why Labour is the Starting Point of Capital. In D. Elson (ed.), *Value: The Representation of Labour in Capitalism*. London: CSE Books, p. 53.

35 Critisticuffs, 2014. A Companion to David Harvey's Companion to Marx' Capital, Chapter 1: https://critisticuffs.org/texts/david-harvey.

36 Marx 1976, pp. 179–80.

37 A. Cutler, B. Hindess, P. Hirst and A. Hussain, 1977. *Capital and Capitalism Today*. Vol. I. London: Routledge and Kegan Paul, p. 14; Elson 1979, p. 152.

38 Elson 1979, pp. 152–3.

39 C. Arthur, 1979. Dialectic of the Value-Form. In D. Elson (ed.), *Value: The Representation of Labour in Capitalism*. London: CSE Books, pp. 67–81.

40 Heinrich 2017, p. 126.

41 Heinrich 2012, pp. 53–5.

42 Marx, MEGA 11/6, p. 31, quoted in Heinrich 2017, p. 126; Heinrich and Wei 2012, p. 727; Marx 1970, p. 88.

43 Marx, 1976, p. 54.

44 Marx 1976, p. 45; W. Bonefeld, 2010. Abstract Labour: Against its Nature and on its Time. *Capital & Class*, 34(2), pp. 257–76 (p. 265).

45 Marx, *Erstausgabe des Kapitals*, quoted in Reichelt 2005, p. 50.

46 K. Marx, 1970. *Contribution to the Critique of Political Economy*. London: Lawrence & Wishart, pp. 50, 57–9.

47 E. von Bohm-Bawerk, 1949. *Karl Marx and the Close of his System*. Auburn, AL: Ludwig von Mises Institute.

48 Kay 1979, pp. 46–66 (p. 54).

49 Elson 1979, p. 151.

50 Heinrich 2012, p. 50.

51 Mirowski 1989, pp. 181–2.

52 Marx 1976, p. 677.

53 M. de Vroey, 1981. Value, Production and Exchange. In I. Steedman (ed.), *The Value Controversy*. London: Verso, pp. 173–201 (p. 176).

54 R. Kurz, 1999. *Marx 2000*: www.exit-online.org, p. 5.

55 Aumeeruddy and Tortajada 1979, pp. 6–7; T. W. Adorno, 1990. *Negative Dialectics*. Trans. E. B. Ashton. London: Routledge.

56 A. Sohn-Rethel, 1978. *Intellectual and Manual Labour*. London: Macmillian, p. 20.

57 Heinrich 2012, pp. 53–5.

58 Bellofiore and Riva 2015, pp. 29–31; A. Kicillof and G.

Starosta, 2007. Value Form and Class Struggle: A Critique of the Autonomist Theory of Value. *Capital & Class*, 92, pp. 13–40.

59 De Vroey 1981, p. 176.
60 Mirowski 1989, pp. 181–2.
61 Marx 1976, pp. 676–7; K. Marx, 1991. *Capital*. Vol. III. London: Penguin, p. 238.
62 Marx 1976, p. 301.
63 Bonefeld 2010, pp. 268–9; C. Arthur, 2013. The Practical Truth of Abstract Labour. In R. Bellofiore, G. Starosta and P. Thomas (eds.), *In Marx's Laboratory: Critical Interpretations of the Grundrisse*. Leiden: Brill, pp. 101–20; H. Cleaver, 2000. *Reading* Capital *Politically*. Edinburgh: AK Press, p. 119.
64 Marx 1976, p. 156; S. Himmelweit and S. Mohun, 1981. Real Abstractions and Anomalous Assumptions. In I. Steedman (ed.), *The Value Controversy*. London: New Left Books, pp. 224–65 (p. 225).
65 Bellofiore and Riva 2015, pp. 29–31; Kicillof and Starosta 2007.
66 Marx 1976, p. 202.
67 Mirowski 1989, p. 408, n. 5.
68 Reichelt 2005, p. 51.
69 Marx 1976, p. 129; amendments and emphasis, Reichelt 2005, p. 51.
70 Reichelt 2005, p. 51.
71 A. Bowie, 2010. *German Philosophy*. Oxford University Press, p. 64.
72 Backhaus 1980; P. Murray, 2013. Unavoidable Crises: Reflections on Backhaus and the Development of Marx's Value-Form Theory in the *Grundrisse*. In R. Bellofiore, G. Starosta and P. Thomas (eds.), *In Marx's Laboratory: Critical Interpretations of the Grundrisse*. Leiden: Brill, pp. 121–46 (p. 124), emphasis added; Himmelweit and Mohun, 1981, p. 234.
73 See Marx 1970, p. 100.
74 De Vroey 1981, p. 189, n. 24.
75 Marx 1970, p. 101.
76 Marx 1970, pp. 91, 100.
77 R. Kurz, 2016. *The Substance of Capital*. Trans. R. Halpin. London: Chronos, p. 192.
78 Kurz 2016, p. 96.
79 Kurz 2016, p. 196.

80 Kurz 2016, p. 206.
81 Kurz 2016, pp. 212–13.
82 Kurz 2016, pp. 193–4, 196–7.
83 Kurz 2016, p. 210.
84 Kurz 2016, pp. 190–1.
85 Heinrich, *Science of Value*, cited in Kurz 2016, pp. 206–7.
86 Kurz 2016, p. 186.
87 Heinrich 2012, pp. 185–91; M. Postone, 2006. History and Helplessness: Mass Mobilization and Contemporary Forms of Anticapitalism. *Public Culture*, 18(1), pp. 93–110; W. Bonefeld, 2019. Critical Theory and the Critique of Antisemitism: On Society as Economic Object. *The Journal of Social Justice*, 9, pp. 1–20; M. Stoetzler, 2019. Capitalism, the Nation and Societal Corrosion: Notes on 'Left-Wing Antisemitism'. *The Journal of Social Justice*, 9, pp. 1–45. On Kurz, see E. Leslie, 2014. Satanic Mills: On Robert Kurz. *Historical Materialism*, 22(3–4), pp. 408–23.
88 For a summary, see M. Bolton and F. H. Pitts, 2018. *Corbynism: A Critical Approach*. Bingley: Emerald, ch. 6.
89 M. Postone, 2003. The Holocaust and the Trajectory of the Twentieth Century. In M. Postone and E. Santner, *Catastrophe and Meaning: The Holocaust and the Twentieth Century*. University of Chicago Press, pp. 81–114; F. Fanon, 1986. *Black Skins, White Masks*. London: Pluto Press; H. White, 2020. How Is Capitalism Racial? Fanon, Critical Theory and the Fetish of Antiblackness. *Social Dynamics: A Journal of African Studies*, DOI: 10.1080/02533952.2020.1758871.
90 White 2020, pp. 2–3, 7, 9–11.
91 White 2020, pp. 2–3.
92 White 2020, p. 10.
93 Fanon 1986, pp. 125–7.
94 White 2020, pp. 9–12.
95 White, 2020, pp. 2–3, p. 9, pp. 11–12.

3 Value as Utility

1 P. Mirowski, 1989. *More Heat than Light: Economics as Social Physics, Physics as Nature's Economics*. Cambridge University Press, p. 202.
2 P. Mirowski, 1990. Learning the Meaning of a Dollar: Conservation Principles and the Social Theory of Value in Economic Theory. *Social Research*, 57(3), pp. 689–717 (p. 698);

J. Viner, 1925. The Utility Theory and Its Critics. *Journal of Political Economy*, 33, pp, 369–87.

3 R. L. Heilbroner, 1983. The Problem of Value in the Constitution of Economic Thought. *Social Research*, 50(2), pp. 253–77 (p. 272).

4 W. S. Jevons, 1970 [1871]. *The Theory of Political Economy*. London: Penguin, p. 186; G. J. Stigler, 1950a. The Development of Utility Theory I. *Journal of Political Economy*, 58(4), pp. 307–27 (p. 316).

5 Heilbroner 1983, p. 272.

6 Mirowski 1989, p. 196.

7 M. Mazzucato, 2019. *The Value of Everything: Making and Taking in the Global Economy*. London: Penguin, p. 60.

8 Mazzucato 2019, p. 65.

9 A. Smith, 1982. *The Wealth of Nations*. London: Penguin, pp. 131–2.

10 Stigler 1950a, p. 308.

11 D. Ricardo, 1981. *The Works and Correspondence of David Ricardo*. Vol I, ed. P. Sraffa and M. Dobb. Cambridge University Press, p. 429; see also Stigler 1950a, p. 311.

12 A. Marshall, 2009 [1890]. *Principles of Economics*. New York: Cosimo, p. 670; Stigler 1950a, pp. 311–12.

13 D. Bernoulli, 1955 [1738]. Exposition of a New Theory on the Measurement of Risk. *Econometrica*, 22, pp. 23–36; J. Nitzan and S. Bichler, 2009. *Capital as Power: A Study of Order and Creorder*. Abingdon: Routledge, p. 128.

14 G. J. Stigler, 1950b. The Development of Utility Theory II. *Journal of Political Economy*, 58(5), pp. 373–96 (pp. 374–5, 390).

15 Marshall, quoted in Stigler 1950b, p. 376.

16 J. Bentham, 1825. *The Rationale of Reward*. London: John and H. T. Hunt, Nitzan and Bichler 2009, p. 128.

17 Stigler 1950a, p. 309.

18 J. Bentham, 1931. *Theory of Legislation*. London: Kegan Paul, p. 103; Stigler 1950a, p. 309.

19 Stigler 1950a, p. 309.

20 Bentham quoted in Stigler 1950a, p. 310.

21 Stigler 1950a, p. 310.

22 Quoted in Stigler 1950a, pp. 313–14.

23 Mirowski 1989, p. 206.

24 Mirowski 1989, pp. 206–7.

25 Jevons 1970 [1871], pp. 128–31.

26 G. Debreu, 1959. *The Theory of Value*. New Haven: Yale University Press; Mirowski 1990, p. 692.
27 Mazzucato 2019, pp. 61, 78.
28 E. Wilson, 2003. To the Finland Station: A Study in the Writing and Acting of History. *New York Review of Books*, p. 293.
29 Quoted in Stigler 1950a, p. 315; H. H. Gossen, 1983. *The Laws of Human Relations*. Cambridge, MA: MIT Press.
30 Mirowski 1989, p. 211.
31 Mirowski 1989, pp. 213–14.
32 Gossen 1983, p. 102.
33 Mirowski 1989, pp. 214–15.
34 Heilbroner 1983, p. 262.
35 Jevons 1970 [1871], p. 187; see Heilbroner 1983, p. 262.
36 Mirowski 1989, pp. 214–15.
37 I. Fisher, 1965 [1892]. *Mathematical Investigations in the Theory of Value and Price, Appreciation and Interest*. New York: A. M. Kelley; Nitzan and Bichler 2009, p. 128.
38 Stigler 1950b, p. 378.
39 Nitzan and Bichler 2009.
40 Fisher 1965 [1892], p. 18.
41 Stigler 1950a, p. 324.
42 Mirowski 1989, p. 196, p. 231.
43 Mirowski 1989, p. 218.
44 Mirowski 1989, p. 231.
45 Mirowski 1989, p. 215.
46 Nitzan and Bichler 2009, p. 129.
47 E. H. Weber, 1978 [1834]. *The Sense of Touch*. New York: Academic Press; G. T. Fechner, 1966 [1860]. *Elements of Psychophysics*. New York: Holt, Rinehart and Winston.
48 D. Kahneman, 2012. *Thinking, Fast and Slow*. London: Penguin, p. 272.
49 D. Colander, 2007. Edgeworth's Hedonimeter and the Quest to Measure Utility. *Journal of Economic Perspectives*, 21(1), pp. 215–26.
50 Kahneman 2012, p. 272.
51 Colander 2007.
52 Kahneman 2012, p. 272.
53 Colander 2007.
54 Wilson 2003, p. 291.
55 F. Y. Edgeworth, 1967 [1881]. *Mathematical Psychics: An Essay on the Application of Mathematics to the Moral Sciences*. New York: A. M. Kelley; Nitzan and Bichler 2009, p. 129.
56 Stigler 1950b, p. 395.

57 Colander 2007.
58 Colander 2007.
59 Fisher 1965 [1892].
60 Fisher, quoted in Colander 2007.
61 Mirowski 1989, pp. 218–19.
62 W. S. Jevons, 1970 [1905]. *Principles of Economics*. New York: A. M. Kelley, p. 50; Mirowski 1989, p. 219.
63 Jevons 1970 [1871]; Nitzan and Bichler 2009, p. 129.
64 Stigler 1950a, p. 317.
65 Jevons 1970 [1871], p. 83; Mirowski 1989, p. 234.
66 Nitzan and Bichler 2009, p. 6.
67 Stigler 1950b, p. 382.
68 Nitzan and Bichler 2009, p. 7.
69 P. A. Samuelson, 1938. A Note on the Pure Theory of Consumer's Behaviour. *Economica*, 5, pp. 61–71; Nitzan and Bichler 2009, p. 130.
70 J. Robinson, 1962. *Economic Philosophy*. London: Penguin, p. 48.
71 Marshall 2009 [1980], p. 78.
72 Nitzan and Bichler 2009, p. 130; Marshall, quoted in Stigler 1950b, p. 383.
73 Pareto, quoted in Stigler 1950b, p. 381; Mirowski 1989, p. 246.
74 Stigler 1950b, pp. 390–1.
75 James, quoted in Stigler 1950b, p. 394.
76 Kahneman 2012; D. Kahneman and J. L. Knetsch, 1992. Valuing Public Goods: The Purchase of Moral Satisfaction. *Journal of Environmental Economics and Management*, 22, pp. 57–70; D. Kahneman and A. Tversky, 1984. Choices, Values and Frames. *American Psychologist*, 34, pp. 341–50; A. Tversky and D. Kahneman, 1974. Judgment under Uncertainty: Heuristics and Biases. *Science*, 185, pp. 1124–31; P. Diamond and J. Hausman, 1994. Contingent Valuation: Is Some Number Better than None? *Journal of Economic Perspectives*, 8(4), pp. 45–64; J. Hausman, 2012. Contingent Valuation: From Dubious to Hopeless. *Journal of Economic Perspectives*, 26(4), pp. 43–56.
77 Nitzan and Bichler 2009, p. 135.
78 Colander 2007.
79 M. Weber, 1975 [1908]. Marginal Utility Theory and 'The Fundamental Law of Psychophysics'. *Social Science Quarterly*, 56, pp. 24–36. So far as we know, the sociologist was no relation to the eponymous 'Weber'.

80 M. Zafirovski, 2001. Max Weber's Analysis of Marginal Utility Theory and Psychology Revisited: Latent Propositions in Economic Sociology and the Sociology of Economics. *History of Political Economy*, 33(3), pp. 437–58 (p. 438).

81 Weber, 1975 [1908]; Zafirovski 2001.

82 Stigler 1950b, p. 377; see M. Weber, 2013. *The Protestant Ethic and the Spirit of Capitalism*. Routledge; P. J. DiMaggio and W. W. Powell, 1983. The Iron Cage Revisited: Collective Rationality and Institutional Isomorphism in Organizational Fields. *American Sociological Review*, 48(2), pp. 147–60; J. R. Barker, 1993. Tightening the Iron Cage: Concertive Control in Self-managing Teams. *Administrative Science Quarterly*, 38(4), pp. 408–37; R. Greenwood and T. B. Lawrence, 2005. The Iron Cage in the Information Age: The Legacy and Relevance of Max Weber for Organization Studies. Editorial. *Organizational Studies*, 26(4), pp. 493–9.

83 Zafirovski 2001, p. 438.

84 Zafirovski 2001, p. 442.

85 Zafirovski 2001, p. 450.

86 Weber 1975 [1908], p. 33.

87 Zafirovski 2001, p. 445.

88 Mirowski 1989, p. 229.

89 Mirowski 1989, p. 250.

90 Stigler 1950b, p. 380.

91 F. H. Pitts, 2015. Creative Industries, Value Theory and Michael Heinrich's New Reading of Marx. *tripleC: Communication, Capitalism and Critique*, 13(1), pp. 192–222.

92 Mazzucato 2019, p. 66.

93 M. Bolton and F. H. Pitts, 2018. *Corbynism: A Critical Approach*. Bingley: Emerald, ch. 1. On the contemporary 'political vernaculars' of 'value creation', see F. Muniesa, 2017. On the Political Vernaculars of Value Creation. *Science as Culture*, 26(4), pp. 445–54.

94 Heilbroner 1983, pp. 273–4.

95 Mazzucato 2019, pp. 69, 241.

96 Mazzucato 2019, p. 65.

97 Heinrich, *Science of Value*, cited in R. Kurz, 2016. *The Substance of Capital*. Trans. R. Halpin. London: Chronos, pp. 206–7.

4 Value and Institutions

1 P. Mirowski, 1990. Learning the Meaning of a Dollar: Conservation Principles and the Social Theory of Value in Economic Theory. *Social Research*, 57(3), pp. 689–717 (pp. 699–700).

2 Mirowski 1990, p. 717.

3 J. Schumpeter, 1954. *History of Economic Analysis*. New York: Oxford University Press, p. 60.

4 C. Castoriadis, 1984. Value, Equality, Justice, Politics: From Marx to Aristotle and from Aristotle to Ourselves. In *Crossroads in the Labyrinth*. Brighton: Harvester Press, pp. 260–339.

5 J. Nitzan and S. Bichler, 2009. *Capital as Power: A Study of Order and Creorder*. Abingdon: Routledge, pp. 7, 148–9.

6 P. Mirowski, 1989. *More Heat than Light: Economics as Social Physics, Physics as Nature's Economics*. Cambridge University Press, pp. 145–6.

7 R. L. Heilbroner, 1983. The Problem of Value in the Constitution of Economic Thought. *Social Research*, 50(2), pp. 253–77 (p. 257).

8 For overviews, see D. Cefai, B. Zimmermann, S. Nicolae and M. Endress, 2015. Introduction to Special Issue on Sociology of Valuation and Evaluation. *Human Studies*, 38, pp. 1–12; A. Kruger and M. Reinhart, 2017. Theories of Valuation – Building Blocks for Conceptualizing Valuation Between Practice and Structure. *Historical Social Research*, 42, pp. 263–85; M. Lamont, 2012. Toward a Comparative Sociology of Valuation and Evaluation. *Annual Review of Sociology*, 38, pp. 201–21. For examples of the approach in action, see M. Fourcade, 2011. Cents and Sensibility: Economic Valuation and the Nature of 'Nature'. *American Journal of Sociology*, 116(6), pp. 1721–77; M. Fourcade, 2011. Price and Prejudice: On Economics and the Enchantment (or Disenchantment) of Nature. In J. Beckert and P. Aspers, *The Worth of Goods: Valuation and Pricing in the Economy*. New York: Oxford University Press, pp. 41–62.

9 Mirowski 1989, pp. 400–1; Mirowski 1990, p. 700; see T. Veblen, 1953. *The Theory of the Leisure Class*. New York: Mentor; W. Sombart, 1967. *Luxury and Capitalism*. Ann Arbor: University of Michigan Press; J. R. Commons, 1968. *The Legal Foundations of Capitalism*. Madison: University of Wisconsin Press.

10 Mirowski 1990, pp. 695, 708.

11 M. Douglas, 1986. *How Institutions Think*. Syracuse University Press, p. 48, p. 58; Mirowski 1989, p. 397.
12 Mirowski 1990, pp. 704–5; see Veblen 1953.
13 Mirowski 1990, pp. 708–9; P. Mirowski, 1991. Postmodernism and the Social Theory of Value. *Journal of Post Keynesian Economics*, 13(4), pp. 565–82 (pp. 568–9).
14 Mirowski 1990, pp. 708–9; Mirowski 1991, pp. 568–9.
15 Commons 1968; Mirowski 1990, p. 706.
16 Mirowski 1990, pp. 709–10.
17 Mirowski 1991, p. 572.
18 Mirowski 1991, pp. 579–80.
19 Nitzan and Bichler 2009, pp. 322–3.
20 T. Veblen, 2007. *Absentee Ownership: Business Enterprise in Recent Times: The Case of America*. Piscataway, NJ: Transaction Publishers.
21 Nitzan and Bichler 2009, pp. 219–20.
22 Nitzan and Bichler 2009, p. 223.
23 Nitzan and Bichler 2009, pp. 17–19.
24 Nitzan and Bichler 2009, p. 218.
25 Heilbroner 1983, p. 258.
26 For pragmatism, see F. Muniesa, 2012. A Flank Movement in the Understanding of Valuation. *Sociological Review*, 2012, pp. 24–38. For deployment of poststructuralist concepts, see I. Hardie and D. MacKenzie, 2007. Assembling an Economic Actor: The Agencement of a Hedge Fund. *Sociological Review*, 55(1), pp. 57–80. For French critical sociology, see L. Boltanski and L. Thevenot, 2006. *On Justification: Economies of Worth*. Princeton University Press. For the practice turn, see K. Knorr-Cetina and E. von Savigny, 2000. *The Practice Turn in Contemporary Theory*. London: Routledge.
27 A. Appadurai, 1986. Introduction: Commodities and the Politics of Value. In A. Appadurai (ed.), *The Social Life of Things: Commodities in Cultural Perspective*. Cambridge University Press, pp. 3–63.
28 G. Simmel, 1978. *The Philosophy of Money*. Trans. T. Bottomore and D. Frisby. London: Routledge.
29 Appadurai 1986, p. 3.
30 Appadurai 1986, p. 57.
31 Appadurai 1986, pp. 3–4.
32 Simmel 1978, p. 80.
33 Appadurai 1986, p. 5.
34 Simmel 1978, p. 138; Appadurai 1986, p. 17, p. 59, n. 4.
35 Simmel 1978, p. 80.

36 Appadurai 1986, pp. 13–14.
37 F. Muniesa, Y. Millo and M. Callon, 2007. An Introduction to Market Devices. In M. Callon, Y. Millo and F. Muniesa (eds.), *Market Devices*. Oxford: Blackwell, pp. 1–13.
38 J. Dewey, 1966. *Theory of Valuation*. University of Chicago Press.
39 Muniesa et al. 2007, p. 1.
40 D. Beunza and D. Stark, 2004. Tools of the Trade: The Socio-Technology of Arbitrage in a Wall Street Trading Room. *Industrial and Corporate Change*, 13(2), pp. 369–400; W. N. Espeland and M. L. Stevens, 1998. Commensuration as a Social Process. *Annual Review of Sociology*, 24, pp. 313–43; F. Cooren, 2004. Textual Agency: How Texts Do Things in Organizational Settings. *Organization*, 11(3), pp. 373–93.
41 D. Beunza, I. Hardie and D. MacKenzie, 2006. A Price Is a Social Thing: Towards a Material Sociology of Arbitrage. *Organization Studies*, 27(5), pp. 721–45; M. Callon and F. Muniesa, 2005. Economic Markets as Calculative Collective Devices. *Organization Studies*, 26(8), pp. 1229–50.
42 Muniesa et al. 2007, p. 2.
43 Muniesa et al. 2007; F. Cochoy and C. Grandclément-Chaffy, 2005, Publicizing Goldilocks' Choice at the Supermarket: The Political Work of Shopping Packs, Carts and Talk. In B. Latour and P. Weibel (eds.), *Making Things Public: Atmospheres of Democracy*. Karlsruhe, Cambridge, MA, and London: ZKM – The MIT Press, pp. 646–59; A. Preda, 2006. Socio-technical Agency in Financial Markets: The Case of the Stock Ticker. *Social Studies of Science*, 36(5), pp. 753–82.
44 Callon and Muniesa 2005; Muniesa et al. 2007, pp. 4–5.
45 Muniesa et al. 2007, p. 5.
46 J. Matthews and J. Smith Maguire (2014). Introduction: Thinking with Cultural Intermediaries. In J. Smith Maguire and J. Matthews (eds.), *The Cultural Intermediaries Reader*. London: SAGE, pp. 1–11 (p. 10); S. Nixon, 2014. Cultural Intermediaries or Market Device? The Case of Advertising. In J. Smith Maguire and J. Matthews (eds.), *The Cultural Intermediaries Reader*. London: SAGE, p. 37.
47 P. Bourdieu, 1984. *Distinction*. Trans. R. Nice. London: Routledge and Kegan Paul. The rest of this section draws upon material first published as F. H. Pitts, 2015. The Cultural Intermediaries Reader. *Cultural Trends*, 24(4), pp. 330–3.
48 Bourdieu 1984, p. 359.
49 L. McFall, 2014. The Problem of Cultural Intermediaries in the

Economy of Qualities. In J. Smith Maguire and J. Matthews (eds.), *The Cultural Intermediaries Reader*. London: SAGE, pp. 42–51 (pp. 44–6).

50 Matthews and Smith Maguire 2014, p. 10.

51 Nixon 2014, p. 38.

52 Matthews and Smith Maguire 2014, p. 10.

53 B. Fine, 2003. Callonistics: A Disentanglement. *Economy and Society*, 32(3), pp. 478–84; A. Whittle and A. Spicer, 2008. Is Actor Network Theory Critique? *Organization Studies*, 29(4), pp. 611–29; J. M. Roberts, 2012. Poststructuralism against Poststructuralism: Actor–Network Theory, Organizations and Economic Markets. *European Journal of Social Theory*, 15(1), pp. 35–53.

54 J. Smith Maguire, 2014. Bourdieu on Cultural Intermediaries. In J. Smith Maguire and J. Matthews (eds.), *The Cultural Intermediaries Reader*. London: SAGE, pp. 15–24 (p. 19).

55 Smith Maguire 2014, p. 23

56 W. Bonefeld, 2014. *Critical Theory and the Critique of Political Economy: On Subversion and Negative Reason*. London: Bloomsbury, p. 119, n. 45.

57 E. B. Weininger, 2005. Foundations of Pierre Bourdieu's Class Analysis.   In Erik Olin Wright (ed.), *Approaches to Class Analysis*.   Cambridge University Press, pp. 120–1, p. 132.

58 Bourdieu 1984. See also F. H. Pitts, 2017. *Critiquing Capitalism Today: New Ways to Read Marx*. New York: Palgrave, pp. 122–6.

59 M. Savage, F. Devine, N. Cunningham et al., 2013. A New Model of Social Class: Findings from the BBC's Great British Class Survey Experiment. *Sociology*, 47(2), pp. 219–50.

60 A. Toscano and J. Woodcock, 2015. Spectres of Marxism: A Comment on Mike Savage's Market Model of Class Difference. *The Sociological Review*, 63, pp. 512–23 (p. 519).

61 D. Gartman, 2012. Bourdieu and Adorno: Converging Theories of Culture and Inequality. *Theory and Society*, 41, pp. 41–72 (p. 58).

62 M. Heinrich, 2012. *An Introduction to the Three Volumes of Karl Marx's* Capital. Trans. A. Locascio. New York: Monthly Review Press, pp. 172–4; K. Marx, 1991. *Capital*. Vol. III. London: Penguin, p. 350.

63 M. Heinrich, 2013. Crisis Theory, the Law of the Tendency of the Profit Rate to Fall, and Marx's Studies in the 1870s. *Monthly Review*, April 2013, pp. 15–32 (pp. 25–6).

64 Nixon 2014, p. 41.

65 M. Mazzucato, 2019. *The Value of Everything: Making and Taking in the Global Economy*. London: Penguin, pp. 7–8, 15.
66 E. Wilson, 2003. To the Finland Station: A Study in the Writing and Acting of History. *New York Review of Books*, p. 294.
67 Mazzucato 2019, p. 11.
68 R. Kurz, 2016. *The Substance of Capital*. Trans. R. Halpin. London: Chronos, p. 186; R. Scholz, 2015. Patriarchy and Commodity Society: Gender without the Body. In N. Larsen, M. Nilges, J. Robinson and N. Brown (eds.), *Marxism and the Critique of Value*. Chicago: MCM, pp. 123–42.
69 Mazzucato 2019, pp. 11, 14, 75.
70 Mazzucato 2019, pp. 13, 76, 100.
71 Mazzucato 2019, pp. 74–6.
72 See M. Bolton and F. H. Pitts, 2018. *Corbynism: A Critical Approach*. Bingley: Emerald, ch. 1.
73 Mazzucato 2019, p. 16.
74 Mazzucato 2019, p. 27.
75 G. M. Tamas, 2009. Telling the Truth About Class. *Socialist Register*, 42, pp. 228–68.
76 Bonefeld 2014, p. 197.
77 W. Bonefeld, 2016. 'Bringing Critical Theory Back In at a Time of Misery: Three Beginnings Without Conclusion'. *Capital & Class*, 40(2), pp. 233–44 (p. 239).
78 J. Abromeit, 2016. Critical Theory and the Persistence of Right-Wing Populism. *Logos: A Journal of Modern Society & Culture*, 15(2–3): http://logosjournal.com/2016/abromeit.
79 T. W. Adorno, 2003. Reflections on Class Theory. In R. Tiedemann (ed.), *Can One Live After Auschwitz? A Philosophical Reader*. Trans. R. Livingstone. Stanford University Press, pp. 93–110 (pp. 96, 99).
80 *Aufheben*, 2017. The Rise of Conspiracy Theories: Reification of Defeat as the Basis of Explanation. *Aufheben*, 24, pp. 12–28 (pp. 15–17).
81 Mazzucato 2019, p. 10. See also F. H. Pitts, 2015. Creative Industries, Value Theory and Michael Heinrich's New Reading of Marx. *tripleC: Communication, Capitalism and Critique*, 13(1), pp. 192–222.
82 Bonefeld 2014, p. 195; Bonefeld 2016, p. 237.
83 Bonefeld 2014, pp. 195–6.
84 K. Marx, 1976. *Capital*. Vol. I. London: Penguin, p. 92.
85 Bonefeld 2014, p. 196.

5 Value as Struggle

1 P. Mirowski, 1989. *More Heat than Light: Economics as Social Physics, Physics as Nature's Economics.* Cambridge University Press.

2 G. Caffentzis, 2005. Immeasurable Value? An Essay on Marx's Legacy. *The Commoner,* 10, pp. 87–114; G. Caffentzis, 2007. Crystals and Analytic Engines: Historical and Conceptual Preliminaries to a New Theory of Machines. *Ephemera: Theory and Politics in Organization,* 7, pp. 24–45.

3 Some passages in this chapter draw from material first published as F. H. Pitts, 2019. Value Form Theory, Open Marxism & the New Reading of Marx. In A. C. Dinerstein, A. G. Vela, E. González and J. Holloway (eds.), *Open Marxism IV: Against a Closing World.* London: Pluto Press. Thanks to David Castle and the publishers for permission to reuse. The chapter also draws, in places, on F. H. Pitts, forthcoming. Measuring and Managing Creative Labour: Value, Time and Billable Hours in the Creative Industries. *Organization.*

4 A. Kicillof and G. Starosta, 2007. Value Form and Class Struggle: A Critique of the Autonomist Theory of Value. *Capital & Class,* 92, pp. 13–40, p. 31, n. 4.

5 For open Marxism, see W. Bonefeld, 2014. *Critical Theory and the Critique of Political Economy: On Subversion and Negative Reason.* London: Bloomsbury; A. Dinerstein, 2015. *The Politics of Autonomy in Latin America: The Art of Organising Hope.* London: Palgrave; J. Holloway, 2002. *Change the World Without Taking Power.* London: Pluto Press; J. Holloway, 2010. *Crack Capitalism.* London: Pluto Press. See A. C. Dinerstein, A. G. Vela, E. González and J. Holloway (eds.), 2019. *Open Marxism IV: Against a Closing World.* London: Pluto Press. For autonomist Marxism, see G. Caffentzis, 2012. *In Letters of Blood and Fire: Work, Machines, and the Crisis of Capitalism.* Oakland: PM Press; H. Cleaver, 2000. *Reading Capital Politically.* Edinburgh: AK Press, p. 129; M. De Angelis, 2007. *The Beginning of History: Value Struggles and Global Capital.* London: Pluto Press.

6 R. Kurz, 2016. *The Substance of Capital.* Trans. R. Halpin. London: Chronos; G. Starosta, 2017. Fetishism and Revolution in the Critique of Political Economy: Critical Reflections on some Contemporary Readings of Marx's Capital. *Continental Thought and Theory,* 1(4), pp. 365–98; Kicillof and Starosta

2007. For more on *Wertkritik*, see N. Larsen, M. Nilges, J. Robinson and N. Brown, 2014. *Marxism and the Critique of Value*. Chicago and Alberta: MCM. For a brief introduction to 'practical criticism', see G. Charnock and G. Starosta, 2016. Introduction: The New International Division of Labour and the Critique of Political Economy Today. In *The New International Division of Labour*. London: Palgrave Macmillan, pp. 1–22.

7　See Cleaver 2000.

8　Endnotes, 2010. Communisation and Value-form Theory. *Endnotes #2: Misery and the Value-form*: https://endnotes.org.uk/issues/2/en/endnotes-communisation-and-value-form-theory.

9　H.-G. Backhaus, 1980. On the Dialectics of the Value-Form. *Thesis Eleven*, 1, pp. 94–119 (p. 99); Bonefeld 2014; R. Bellofiore and T. R. Riva, 2015. The Neue Marx-Lekture: Putting the Critique of Political Economy Back into the Critique of Society. *Radical Philosophy*, 189, pp. 24–36; Bonefeld 2014, pp. 41–2; W. Bonefeld, 2016a. Negative Dialectics and Critique of Economic Objectivity. *History of the Human Sciences*, 29(2), pp. 60–76; W. Bonefeld, 2016b. 'Bringing Critical Theory Back In at a Time of Misery: Three Beginnings Without Conclusion'. *Capital & Class*, 40(2), pp. 233–44.

10　Bonefeld 2014; P. Murray, 2013. Unavoidable Crises: Reflections on Backhaus and the Development of Marx's Value-Form Theory in the *Grundrisse*. In R. Bellofiore, G. Starosta and P. Thomas (eds.), *In Marx's Laboratory: Critical Interpretations of the Grundrisse*. Leiden: Brill, pp. 121–46 (p. 129).

11　M. Postone and T. Brennan, 2009. Labor and the Logic of Abstraction. *South Atlantic Quarterly*, 108(2), pp. 305–30 (p. 310); Backhaus 1980.

12　T. W. Adorno, 2000. *Introduction to Sociology*. Trans. E. Jephcott. Cambridge: Polity, p. 141.

13　Murray 2013, p. 131.

14　R. Gunn, 1987. Marxism and Mediation. *Common Sense*, 2, pp. 57–66 (p. 60); see also R. Gunn, 1992. Against Historical Materialism: Marxism as First-Order Discourse. In W. Bonefeld, R. Gunn and K. Psychopedis (eds.), *Open Marxism II: Theory and Practice*. London: Pluto Press, pp. 1–45; and, A. C. Dinerstein and F. H. Pitts, 2018. From Post-work to Post-capitalism? Discussing the Basic Income and Struggles for Alternative Forms of Social Reproduction. *Journal of Labor & Society*, 21(4), pp. 471–91.

15　T. W. Adorno, 2003. Reflections on Class Theory. In R. Tiedemann (ed.), *Can One Live After Auschwitz? A Philosophical Reader.* Trans. R. Livingstone. Stanford University Press, pp. 93–110 (p. 93).

16 K. Marx, 1970. *Contribution to the Critique of Political Economy.* London: Lawrence & Wishart, p. 22.

17 Gunn 1987.

18 M. Heinrich, 2007. Invaders from Marx: On the Uses of Marxian Theory, and the Difficulties of a Contemporary Reading, *Left Curve*, 31: www.oekonomiekritik.de/205Invaders.htm; A. C. Dinerstein, 2014. Too Bad for the Facts: Confronting Value with Hope (Notes on the Argentine Uprising of 2001). *South Atlantic Quarterly*, 113(2), pp. 367–78; M. Heinrich and X. Wei, 2012. The Interpretation of Capital: An Interview with Michael Heinrich. *World Review of Political Economy*, 2(4), pp. 708–28 (p. 717).

19 K. Marx, 1976. *Capital.* Vol. I. London: Penguin, p. 166.

20 M. Heinrich, forthcoming. *The Science of Value: Marx's Critique of Political Economy Between Scientific Revolution and Classical Tradition.* Trans. A. Locascio. Chicago and Leiden: Haymarket/Brill.

21 Gunn 1987, p. 59.

22 Heinrich and Wei 2012, p. 716.

23 Backhaus 1980, p. 107.

24 Postone and Brennan 2009, p. 313.

25 Marx 1976; J. Holloway, 2015. Read Capital: The First Sentence of *Capital* Starts with Wealth, Not with the Commodity. *Historical Materialism*, 23(3), pp. 3–26.

26 R. Bellofiore, 2009. A Ghost Turning into a Vampire: The Concept of Capital and Living Labour. In R. Bellofiore and R. Fineschi (eds.), *Re-reading Marx: New Perspectives after the Critical Edition.* Basingstoke: Palgrave Macmillan, pp. 178–94.

27 Heinrich forthcoming.

28 Marx 1976, p. 164; Bonefeld 2014, p. 78.

29 Bellofiore and Riva 2015, p. 25.

30 M. Heinrich, 2012. *An Introduction to the Three Volumes of Karl Marx's* Capital. Trans. A. Locascio. New York: Monthly Review Press, p. 92; D. Harvey, 2003. *The New Imperialism.* Oxford University Press; M. De Angelis, 2004. Separating the Doing and the Deed: Capital and the Continuous Character of Enclosures. *Historical Materialism*, 12(2), pp. 57–87.

31 Postone and Brennan 2009, p. 316.

32 T. Bhattacharya, 2017. *Social Reproduction Theory: Remapping Class, Recentering Oppression.* London: Pluto Press; M. Dalla

Costa, 1995. Capitalism and Reproduction. In W. Bonefeld, R. Gunn, J. Holloway and K. Psychopedis (eds.), *Open Marxism III: Emancipating Marx*. London: Pluto Press, pp. 7–16; G. Caffentzis, 2002. On the Notion of a Crisis of Social Reproduction: A Theoretical Review. *The Commoner*, 5, pp. 1–22; S. Federici, 2012. *Revolution at Point Zero: Housework, Reproduction, and Feminist Struggle*. Oakland: PM Press; L. Fortunati, 1995. *The Arcane of Reproduction: Housework, Prostitution, Labor and Capital*. New York: Autonomedia.

33 M. De Angelis, 1995. Beyond the Technological and the Social Paradigms: A Political Reading of Abstract Labour as the Substance of Value. *Capital & Class*, 19(3), pp. 107–34 (p. 122).

34 S. Ferguson and D. McNally, 2015. Social Reproduction Beyond Intersectionality: An Interview. *Viewpoint Magazine*, 5: https://viewpointmag.com/2015/10/31/social-reproduction-beyond-intersectionality-an-interview-with-sue-ferguson-and-david-mcnally; L. Vogel, 2013. *Marxism and the Oppression of Women: Toward a Unitary Theory*. Leiden: Brill.

35 C. Robinson, 1983. *Black Marxism*. Chapel Hill: University of North Carolina Press; O. Patterson, 1977. Slavery. *Annual Review of Sociology*, 3, pp. 407–49; F. Wilderson III, 2003. Gramsci's Black Marx: Whither the Slave in Civil Society? *Social Identities*, 9(2), pp. 225–40; S. Issar, 2020. Listening to Black Lives Matter: Racial Capitalism and the Critique of Neoliberalism. *Contemporary Political Theory*, DOI: 1 0.1057/s41296-020-00399-0; H. White, 2020. How Is Capitalism Racial? Fanon, Critical Theory and the Fetish of Antiblackness. *Social Dynamics: A Journal of African Studies*, DOI: 10.1080/02533952.2020.1758871.

36 S. M. Sorentino, 2019a. The Abstract Slave: Anti-Blackness and Marx's Method. *International Labor and Working-Class History*, 96, pp. 17–37 (p. 18).

37 S. M. Sorentino, 2019b. Natural Slavery, Real Abstraction, and the Virtuality of Anti-Blackness. *Theory & Event*, 22(3), pp. 630–73 (p. 631); J. Clegg and R. Lucas, 2015. Brown v. Ferguson. *Endnotes*, 4, pp. 10–69.

38 J. Melamed, 2015. Racial Capitalism. *Critical Ethnic Studies*, 1(1), pp. 76–85 (p. 77).

39 C. Chen, 2013. The Limit Point of Capitalist Equality: Notes Toward an Abolitionist Antiracism. *Endnotes*, 3, pp. 202–23.

40 Banaji, quoted in Sorentino 2019a, p. 22.

41 Sorentino 2019a, pp. 20, 23, 25, 27.

42 Kicillof and Starosta 2007, p. 31, n. 4; De Angelis, 1995.
43 Backhaus 1980, p. 101; Heinrich 2012, pp. 45–7.
44 D. Elson, 1979. The Value Theory of Labour. In D. Elson (ed.), *Value: The Representation of Labour in Capitalism*. London: CSE Books, pp. 115–80.
45 K. Marx, 1861–3. *Economic and Philosophical Manuscripts*: www.marxists.org/archive/marx/works/1861/economic/ch38. htm.
46 Marx 1976, pp. 168–9.
47 De Angelis 1995, p. 107.
48 Kurz 2016, pp. 200–1.
49 Kicillof and Starosta 2007, pp. 16–17.
50 Kicillof and Starosta 2007, pp. 14–15.
51 De Angelis 1995, pp. 126–7.
52 Kurz 2016, pp. 81, 89–90.
53 De Angelis 1995, p. 110.
54 De Angelis 1995, p. 123.
55 De Angelis 1995, p. 117.
56 Kurz 2016, pp. 198–9, p. 206.
57 Kurz 2016, p. 210.
58 De Angelis 1995, pp. 110–11, 113. See also Kicillof and Starosta 2007, pp. 17–18. For the concept of 'practical abstraction', see C. Arthur, 2013. The Practical Truth of Abstract Labour. In R. Bellofiore, G. Starosta and P. Thomas (eds.), *In Marx's Laboratory: Critical Interpretations of the Grundrisse*. Leiden: Brill, pp. 101–20.
59 D. Harvie and K. Milburn, 2010. How Organizations Value and How Value Organizes. *Organization*, 17(5), pp. 631–6 (pp. 631–2).
60 Harvie and Milburn 2010, pp. 634–5.
61 Cleaver 2000, pp. 119–21.
62 Cleaver 2000, p. 129.
63 Kurz 2016, pp. 97–111, p. 209.
64 M. De Angelis and D. Harvie, 2009. Cognitive Capitalism and the Rat-Race: How Capital Measures Immaterial Labour in British Universities. *Historical Materialism*, 17(3), pp. 3–30 (pp. 15–16).
65 Holloway 2002, pp. 45–7.
66 S. Tischler, 2005. Time of Reification and Time of Insubordination: Some Notes. In W. Bonefeld and K. Psychopedis (eds.), *Human Dignity: Social Autonomy and the Critique of Capitalism*. Aldershot: Ashgate, pp. 131–43 (pp. 131–5).
67 W. Bonefeld, 2016c. Science, Hegemony and Action: On the

Elements of Governmentality. *Journal of Social Sciences*, 12(2), pp. 19–41.

68 Bonefeld 2016c.

69 T. W. Adorno, 2008. *Lectures on History and Freedom*. Ed. R. Tiedemann. Trans. R. Livingstone. Cambridge: Polity, p. 118.

70 For a demonstration of some differences between open and autonomist Marxism, see W. Bonefeld, 2010. Abstract Labour: Against its Nature and on its Time. *Capital & Class*, 34(2), pp. 257–76.

71 Starosta 2017, p. 376.

72 Kicillof and Starosta 2007, pp. 15–16, 20–3.

73 Starosta 2017, p. 382.

74 Kicillof and Starosta 2007, pp. 23–4.

75 M. Postone, 1993. *Time, Labor, and Social Domination: A Reinterpretation of Marx's Critical Theory*. Cambridge University Press, pp. 314–23.

76 Kurz 2016, p. 177.

77 Starosta 2017, pp. 387–9

6 Value in Crisis

1 In places, this chapter draws upon formulations first published as F. H. Pitts, 2014. Time Crisis: Autonomist Thought, the Immaterial Working Day and the Dot. Com Boom and Bust. *Sociologia del Lavoro*, 2014(133), pp. 171–82; and F. H. Pitts, 2020. The Multitude and the Machine: Populism, Productivism, Posthumanism. *Political Quarterly*, 91(2). Some passages also draw on F. H. Pitts, forthcoming. Measuring and Managing Creative Labour: Value, Time and Billable Hours in the Creative Industries. *Organization*.

2 M. De Angelis, 1995. Beyond the Technological and the Social Paradigms: A Political Reading of Abstract Labour as the Substance of Value. *Capital & Class*, 19(3), pp. 107–34 (p. 119).

3 M. Hardt and A. Negri, 2001. *Empire*. Cambridge, MA: Harvard University Press. See F. H. Pitts, 2017. *Critiquing Capitalism Today: New Ways to Read Marx*. New York: Palgrave; F. H. Pitts, 2018. A Crisis of Measurability? Critiquing Post-Operaismo on Labour, Value and the Basic Income. *Capital & Class*, 42(1), pp. 3–21.

4 M. Lazzarato, 1996. Immaterial Labor. In P. Virno and M. Hardt (eds.), *Radical Thought in Italy*. Minneapolis: University of Minnesota Press, pp. 133–50.

5 Hardt and Negri 2001; C. Marazzi, 2008. *Capital and Language*. Los Angeles: Semiotext(e); C. Vercellone, 2010. The Crisis of the Law of Value and the Becoming-Rent of Profit. In A. Fumagalli and S. Mezzadra (eds.), *Crisis in the Global Economy*. Los Angeles: Semiotext(e), pp. 85–118.

6 K. Marx, 1993. *Grundrisse*. London: Penguin. See F. H. Pitts, 2017. Beyond the Fragment: Postoperaismo, Postcapitalism and Marx's 'Notes on Machines', 45 Years On. *Economy and Society*, 46(3–4), pp. 324–45.

7 M. Hardt and A. Negri, 2017. *Assembly*. Oxford University Press, pp. 164–5.

8 Hardt and Negri 2017, pp. 143–6.

9 Hardt and Negri 2017, p. 185.

10 A. Beverungen, S. Böhm and C. Land, 2015. Free Labour, Social Media, Management: Challenging Marxist Organization Studies. *Organization Studies*, 36(4), pp. 473–89 (pp. 473–4).

11 Hardt and Negri 2017, p. 175.

12 Hardt and Negri 2017, p. 173.

13 S. Boehm and C. Land, 2009. No Measure for Culture? Value in the New Economy. *Capital & Class*, 97, pp. 75–98 (p. 90); E. Dowling, R. Nunes and B. Trott, 2007. Immaterial and Affective Labour. *ephemera*, 7(1), pp. 1–7; A. Arvidsson, 2010. The Ethical Economy: New Forms of Value in the Information Society? *Organization*, 17(5), p. 637–44; S. Boehm and C. Land, 2012. The New 'Hidden Abode': Reflections on Value and Labour in the New Economy. *Sociological Review*, 60(2), pp. 217–40; Beverungen et al., 2015; P. Mason, 2019. *Clear Bright Future*. London: Allen Lane; A. Bastani, 2019. *Fully Automated Luxury Communism*. London: Verso.

14 H. Willmott, 2010. Creating 'Value' Beyond the Point of Production: Branding, Financialization and Market Capitalization. *Organization*, 17(5), pp. 517–42 (pp. 517–18).

15 Willmott 2010, p. 521.

16 Beverungen et al. 2015, p. 473.

17 C. Marazzi, 2010. *The Violence of Financial Capitalism*. Los Angeles: Semiotext(e), p. 56.

18 M. Hardt and A. Negri, 2009. *Commonwealth*. Cambridge, MA: Harvard University Press, pp. 135–6.

19 Vercellone 2010, pp. 110–11.

20 Hardt and Negri 2001.

21 Hardt and Negri 2017, p. 213.

22 Hardt and Negri 2017, p. 165.

23 Arvidsson 2010, p. 641.

24 For broader perspectives on finance and value, some of which take up the same Foucauldian/Deleuzian theoretical basis as the postoperaists with slightly different effects, see K. Birch, 2017. Rethinking Value in the Bio-Economy: Finance, Assetization, and the Management of Value. *Science, Technology, & Human Values*, 42(3), pp. 460–90; E. Chiapello, 2015. Financialisation of Valuation. *Human Studies*, 38(1), pp. 13–35; M. Feher, 2018. *Rated Agency: Investee Politics in a Speculative Age*. Trans. Gregory Elliot. New York: Zone Books / MIT Press; H. Ortiz, 2013. Financial Value: Economic, Moral, Political, Global. *HAU: Journal of Ethnographic Theory*, 3(1), pp. 64–79; F. Muniesa, L. Doganova, H. Ortiz, et al., 2017. *Capitalization: A Cultural Guide*. Paris: Presses des Mines.

25 Marazzi 2008, p. 43.

26 Marazzi 2008, p. 60.

27 Vercellone 2010, pp. 110–11.

28 A. Fumagalli, 2010. The Global Economic Crisis and Socioeconomic Governance. In *Crisis in the Global Economy: Financial Markets, Social Struggles, and New Political Scenarios*. Los Angeles: Semiotext (e), pp. 61–84 (p. 66).

29 Marazzi 2010, pp. 28–9; Marazzi 2008, p. 14.

30 Marazzi 2008, p. 45.

31 Marazzi 2008, p. 26.

32 Fumagalli 2010, p. 77.

33 Marazzi 2008, p. 34.

34 S. Mezzadra, 2010. Introduction. In A. Fumagalli and S. Mezzadra (eds.), *Crisis in the Global Economy*. Trans. J. F. McGimsey. Los Angeles: Semiotext(e), pp. 7–16 (p. 14).

35 Marazzi 2008, p. 134.

36 Marazzi 2010, p. 49.

37 A. Fumagalli and S. Mezzadra, 2010. Nothing Will Ever Be the Same: Ten Theses on the Financial Crisis. In *Crisis in the Global Economy*. Los Angeles: Semiotext(e), pp. 237–72 (p. 241).

38 Hardt and Negri 2017, p. 159.

39 Vercellone 2010.

40 Arvidsson 2010, p. 637; F. Berardi, 2009. *The Soul at Work: From Alienation to Autonomy*. Los Angeles: Semiotext(e), p. 75.

41 M. De Angelis and D. Harvie, 2009. Cognitive Capitalism and the Rat-Race: How Capital Measures Immaterial Labour in British Universities. *Historical Materialism*, 17(3), pp. 3–30.

42 De Angelis and Harvie 2009, pp. 5–6.

43 De Angelis and Harvie 2009, pp. 26–7.

44 G. Caffentzis, 2005. Immeasurable Value? An Essay on Marx's Legacy. *The Commoner*, 10, pp. 87–114 (p. 97).

45 D. Harvie and K. Milburn, 2010. How Organizations Value and How Value Organizes. *Organization*, 17(5), pp. 631–6 (p. 633).

46 Hardt and Negri 2017, p. 175.

47 Harvie and Milburn 2010; J. Reinecke, 2010. Beyond a Subjective Theory of Value and Towards a 'Fair Price'. *Organization*, 17(5), pp. 563–81 (p. 564).

48 Hardt and Negri 2017, p. 165.

49 K. Marx, 1976. *Capital*. Vol. I. London: Penguin, p. 129.

50 Hardt and Negri 2017, p. 173.

51 Marx 1976, p. 304; C. Arthur, 2013. The Practical Truth of Abstract Labour. In R. Bellofiore, G. Starosta and P. Thomas (eds.), *In Marx's Laboratory: Critical Interpretations of the Grundrisse*. Leiden: Brill, pp. 101–20.

52 See Pitts 2017, 2018.

53 M. Postone and T. Brennan, 2009. Labor and the Logic of Abstraction. *South Atlantic Quarterly*, 108(2), pp. 305–30 (p. 320).

54 H.-G. Backhaus, 1980. On the Dialectics of the Value-Form. *Thesis Eleven*, 1, pp. 94–119 (p. 107).

55 W. Bonefeld, 1987. Marxism and the Concept of Mediation. *Common Sense*, 2, pp. 67–72 (p. 68).

56 M. Heinrich and X. Wei, 2012. The Interpretation of Capital: An Interview with Michael Heinrich. *World Review of Political Economy*, 2(4), pp. 708–28 (p. 716).

57 P. Murray, 2013. Unavoidable Crises: Reflections on Backhaus and the Development of Marx's Value-Form Theory in the *Grundrisse*. In R. Bellofiore, G. Starosta and P. Thomas (eds.), *In Marx's Laboratory: Critical Interpretations of the Grundrisse*. Leiden: Brill, pp. 121–46 (p. 124).

Index